Igor Webb

FROM CUSTOM TO CAPITAL

*The English Novel
and the
Industrial Revolution*

Cornell University Press

Ithaca and London

International Standard Book Number 0-8014-1392-3
Library of Congress Catalog Card Number 81-433
Printed in the United States of America
*Librarians: Library of Congress cataloging information appears
on the last page of the book.*

To my parents

Contents

Preface

THIS book argues that any novel written between roughly 1780 and the 1850s is necessarily an expression of and a response to the events we have come to call, somewhat narrowly, the Industrial Revolution. No claim is made to being comprehensive, however, and I do not consider most of the "industrial" or "social" novels of the period. Instead, to demonstrate the fundamental—rather than casual—interconnections between social consciousness and the forms of fiction, I concentrate on a handful of novels by Jane Austen, Charlotte Brontë, and Charles Dickens.

I discuss Austen's *Pride and Prejudice* and *Mansfield Park*, Brontë's *Jane Eyre* and *Shirley*, and Dickens's more obviously industrial *Hard Times*. In all of these novels the complex and vexing relationship between the history of women's aspirations for fulfillment and the broader history of a society in the process of epochal transformation is thoroughly revealed. I attempt to show, for example, how the contrast between the celebrations of mobility and equality in *Pride and Prejudice* and *Jane Eyre* and the uncomfortable, even hectoring defenses of landed and industrial capitalism in *Mansfield Park* and *Shirley* reflects central aspects of nineteenth-century social consciousness.

9

The formal problem that Austen, Brontë, and Dickens face is the difficulty of assimilating the profoundly disruptive social and political developments of their time into the novel of manners. I pursue this part of my discussion in a speculative analysis of correspondences among courtship, attitudes toward crime and the crowd, and the structure of nineteenth-century English fiction.

Much of this work is exploratory, although it covers familiar ground. I do not mount a polemic for a new theory or method, but rather try to extend the holist tradition of historical and cultural Marxist criticism, the tradition of Georg Lukács, Lucien Goldmann, and Raymond Williams. In my introductory chapter I briefly outline what I take to be the contribution of these critics, as well as my debt to them.

I am also grateful to Basil Blackwell Publishers for permission to quote from *Shirley: A Tale* (1931); Cambridge University Press and Michael Anderson for permission to quote from his *Family Structure in Nineteenth-Century Lancashire* (1971); Jonathan Cape Ltd. and Harcourt Brace Jovanovich for permission to quote from Walter Benjamin, *Illuminations*, trans. Harry Zohn, ed. Hannah Arendt (1968); Lawrence & Wishart Ltd. for permission to quote from Brian Simon, *The Two Nations and the Educational Structure, 1780–1870* (1974); Barclay's Bank Trust Company Ltd. for permission to quote from M. Dorothy George, *London Life in the Eighteenth Century* (1925); Victor Gollancz and Pantheon Books for permission to quote from E. P. Thompson, *The Making of the English Working Class* (1963); Chatto & Windus for permission to quote from Raymond Williams, *The Long Revolution* (1961) and *The English Novel from Dickens to Lawrence* (1974); Pantheon Books and Macmillan Publishers for permission to quote from Michael Ignatieff, *A Just Measure of Pain: The Penitentiary in the Industrial Revolution* (1978); Macmillan Publishers for permission to quote from Terry Eagleton, *Myths of Power: A Marxist Study of the Brontës* (1975); Oxford University Press for permission to quote from R. W. Chapman's editions of *Pride and Prejudice* and *Mansfield Park* (1923, 1966), Margaret Smith's edition of *Jane Eyre* (1973), and Raymond Williams, *Marxism and Literature* (1977); and Weidenfeld (Publishers) Ltd. for permission to quote from Lawrence Stone, *The Family, Sex, and Marriage in England, 1500–1800* (1977; published in the United States by Columbia University Press).

IGOR WEBB

Leigh-on-Sea, Essex, England

FROM CUSTOM
TO CAPITAL

CHAPTER ONE

Introduction: An
Autobiography of Method

ABOUT twenty years ago I chanced to come across Leslie
Stephen's *English Literature and Society in the Eighteenth
Century* (1904). I was reading Virginia Woolf, knew little of
Stephen, and was not much attracted to the English eighteenth
century. But I took the book up anyway and then quickly became convinced of what I continue to believe now—that it is a
minor critical masterpiece. My own literary education in the
late 1950s and early 1960s, at Tufts and Stanford, was dominated by two classroom disciplines: one, an intense application
of close reading derived from T. S. Eliot's most questionable
proposition, that a work of literature is autotelic; and the other
an inexorable insistence on intellectual "background" and
study of "influence," which in practice too often meant the use
of scholarship to protect teacher and student from the experience of reading.[1] This was, I believe, a standard education.
Leslie Stephen's book seemed to come out of a totally different
world; it opened my eyes to the possibility of seeing literature
as an actual social practice of actual people at a particular place
and time. If this is not a revolutionary notion, nonetheless it

1. I grant the exceptions. The outstanding ones, in my case, were Ber-
nard McCabe at Tufts and Yvor Winters, Thomas Moser, and Wilfred
Stone at Stanford.

15

rarely takes shape as an active classroom discipline. And despite the social turmoil of the twenty years since I first read Stephen's book, the situation in college English literature classrooms remains—at heart—basically unchanged. My aim here is still, therefore, much like Stephen's: to show how some works of English literature might be viewed as communications within a particular society. Much recent scholarship has connected industrial novels—those that take industrialism as their subject—and the social, political, and economic events of their time. Although I believe this to be crucial work—and try to do some of it here—I am more interested in demonstrating that *any* novel written between, say, 1780 and the 1850s bears the impress of and is at its core a response to that transformation of society somewhat inaccurately called the Industrial Revolution.

A method that makes this point convincingly must take account of Stephen's book. The greatness of *English Literature and Society in the Eighteenth Century* depends on its elaboration of what Stephen calls "the historical attitude."[2]

> The literary history, as I conceive it, is an account of one strand, so to speak, in a very complex tissue: it is connected with the intellectual and social development; it represents movements of thought which may sometimes check and be sometimes propitious to the existing forms of art; it is the utterance of a class which may represent, or fail to represent, the main national movement; it is affected more or less directly by all manner of religious, political, social, and economic changes; and it is dependent upon the occurrence of individual genius for which we cannot even profess to account. [Pp. 18–19]

This method, in Stephen's graceful, sensible, and honest style, yields him very impressive results, as for example this judgment of Scott: "His masterpieces are not his descriptions of medieval knights so much as the stories in which he illumi-

---

2. Leslie Stephen, *English Literature and Society in the Eighteenth Century* (New York: Barnes & Noble, 1962; first published 1904), p. 2. Further references are cited in the text.

nates the present by his vivid presentation of the present order as the outgrowth from the old, and makes the Scottish peasant or lawyer or laird interesting as a product and a type of social conditions" (p. 131). Writing not as a Marxist but as a liberal, a full thirty years before Georg Lukács's essay on the historical novel (1937), Stephen reveals a quite startling consciousness of historical process and of the writer as the voice of the profound forces of his or her own time. Stephen's insights and method themselves, however, come out of a particular stage of intellectual development in England. They are, necessarily, products of a specific period. There is a kind of unsteadiness about the book. Here Stephen talks of Gothicism and romanticism:

> The indifferent dilettante, caring little for any principles and mainly desirous of amusement, discovers a certain charm in the old institutions while he professes to despise them in theory. That means one of the elements of the complex sentiment which we describe as romanticism. The past is obsolete but pretty enough to be used in making new playthings. The reconciliation will be reached when the growth of historical inquiry leads men to feel that past and present are parts of a continuous series, and to look upon their ancestors neither as simply ridiculous nor as objects of blind admiration. [P. 102]

This passage begins in the way of the literary world, in the tone of a particular sophistication that has nothing to do with historical method. If consciousness is "determined" by "the social movement," then Stephen's talk of indifferent dilettantes out to entertain themselves obviously will not do. It may be amusing, but it does not help us understand the rise of Gothicism. Its failure is precisely its shallow sense of social process and of fundamental forces as they affect, and are affected by, movements in consciousness. Just for this reason the final sentence surprises. It does not seem to have any deep relation to what precedes it, yet it is on the whole just and precise; so that we see Stephen articulating a historical attitude that yet fails to permeate his own way of working.

If we press to discover why this might be so, we come back to his explanation of historical attitude. He offers us the image of "a very complex tissue," and of literature "affected more or less directly by all manner of religious, political, social, and economic changes." Now of course, so far as it goes, this is a true account. But there is a danger that if we look at complexity as Stephen does, the work of literature affected by all manner of things, there is a danger that in following such a method we will fail to see the society at all. If everything is affecting everything else in this way, the real *social* process gets obscured, and one can no longer see it. Absent is any sense of relationships of power, of conflict among classes, of fundamental attitudes and dominant forces—of "the social movement." Of course Stephen names the classes and the movement, and states his sense of determination. But then he cannot enact it because his view of the problem is not coherent and because he lacks a profound account of social development.

This is the difference between Stephen and Lukács. Lukács's advance is absolutely central—though of course not complete. To alter slightly the title of one of his books, he made manifest the relation between history and consciousness. He was able to do so because he was a Marxist. His Marxism gave him two decisive advantages—I take them to be advantages—over Stephen. First, Lukács had recourse to a developed philosophy of social change, specifically an account of capitalist society and of the historical process. Second, Lukács had recourse to the categories of Marxism, specifically the notion of totality. Out of these categories, Lukács developed and applied to literary criticism a category Stephen himself considers: typicality.

Discussions of the "relation" between literature and society tend to focus on precisely this problem of relation: how does being make consciousness? But in reading Stephen one comes across an apparently anterior problem, for Stephen's notion of "social movement" is perplexing. One is hard put to say what, precisely, he has in mind. If one's notion of social being is in this way unformed or awry or in any event inadequate, can one usefully speak of its "relation" to literature or consciousness? It is a debilitating weakness in Stephen's account that his idea of history only casually includes industrial capitalism, and that he sees only vaguely the implications for consciousness of the new modes of production—when he sees them at all. In a discussion of eighteenth-century England these omissions or misperceptions mean an incompleteness in the account of human life—and consequently an inevitable incompleteness of literary understanding.

And this incompleteness of perception leads Stephen to accept as adequate explanations of phenomena which are actually confusing or shallow. His judgment of Scott, for instance, comes at the end of his book when he offers explanation of changes at the turn of the eighteenth century. At this time, he says, "intellectual movement has introduced a new element. The historical sense is being developed, as a settled society with a complex organization becomes conscious at once of its continuity and of the slow processes of growth by which it has been elaborated" (p. 130). Now here a kind of description is substituted for explanation. How is it, one asks, that "intellectual movement" now introduced a new element? What "determined" this intellectual movement?

In Lukács's account of the same development, he asks what Stephen ignores: Why did the historical sense emerge at this particular time? And he seeks for an answer in social conditions. Among his responses is an important analysis of the French Revolution and the Napoleonic wars as *mass* experiences. The total involvement of nations in revolution and war, the development of a mass army, destroyed the notion of history as at once fixed and "natural," and revealed it as a process of change affecting each individual and determined by human activity. In this way history comes for Lukács to be demonstrated as human self-activity, and the activity of the present demonstrated as the precondition of the future. In observing the making of history in this unprecedented way men and women came to the *idea* of history.[3]

We observe, then, a significant difference in method. It is important to say that Lukács was careful to add at this point in his argument that the actual determination of consciousness is an extraordinarily complex process, and not a mechanical one. Partly this awareness became expressed in his thought, especially in his earlier writing, by means of the notion of totality, which itself has two relevant aspects. First, totality stresses the wholesale interaction among factors in the social process, the idea that capitalism, for instance, implies a totality of experience. Second, more powerfully perhaps, Lukács emphasizes the total reverberation in consciousness of basic relationships, centrally distinguishing between the ways in which the bourgeoisie and the working class relate to objects. The worker sees an object as part of the process of, say, production; it is not mysterious, nor is it unknowable. But for the bourgeois the thing-in-itself cannot be known (as in Kant's philosophy). Lukács explains this inability as a function of a class relation to reality.[4] In this way Lukács explores the totality of experience in terms of essential concrete relationships between the individual and his or her actual social world. And such exploration propels Lukács past Stephen's shallow sense both of history and of consciousness. In the final analysis Lukács always returns, as Stephen does only erratically, to the primary stress that being determines consciousness.

For Lukács this relation is most fully and wholly evident in art, which "aspires to maximum profundity and comprehensiveness, at grasping life in its all-embracing totality."[5] The unique power of art is that it "combines the universal, particu-

3. Georg Lukács, *The Historical Novel* (Harmondsworth: Penguin Books, 1969), pp. 20–27.

4., See Fredric Jameson, *Marxism and Form* (Princeton: Princeton University Press, 1971), pp. 184–88.

5. Georg Lukács, *Writer and Critic* (London: Merlin Press, 1970), p. 77.

lar and individual into a dynamic unity."[6] One of the expressions of this unity in literature is "the type." Lukács distinguishes the type from its caricatured "vulgar" manifestations—as in the portrayal of the fat capitalist and so on—and from the naturalistic manifestation of it as "the average."

> What characterizes the type is the convergence and intersection of all the dominant aspects of that dynamic unity through which genuine literature reflects life in a vital and contradictory unity—all the most important social, moral and spiritual contradictions of a time. The representation of the average, on the other hand, inevitably results in diluting and deadening these contradictions, the reflection of the great problems of any age; by being represented in the mind and experiences of an average man, they lose their decisiveness.[7]

Lukács employs this analysis to distinguish between Zola and Balzac, the one a writer of the average and the other of the fundamental. The importance of this category is that it cuts through false distinctions in critical discussion between art and life, form and content. The truly vital art expresses the social process at its deepest level—that is Lukács's point.

But if Lukács transcends Stephen in his conception of historical process, he does not so well address another of Stephen's difficulties, which is his uncertainty about how to state the correspondence between literary consciousness and the broader cultural consciousness. For me, a way to begin to overcome this difficulty is with Lucien Goldmann's restatement of the notion that being determines consciousness. For Goldmann literature is the expression of a vision of the world, and "visions of the world are not individual but social facts."[8] If visions of the world are not individual but social facts, then

6. Ibid.
7. Ibid., p. 78.
8. Lucien Goldmann, "Dialectical Materialism and Literary History," *New Left Review*, no. 92 (July–August 1975), p. 40.

they must be identifiable not just in a novel or a poem but in a commonly held world view. To show how visions of the world are not individual but social I have borrowed a phrase and concept from Raymond Williams: "structure of feeling."

In his early use of this phrase, Williams wanted to reaffirm an emphasis Stephen felt he had to write against, that is, that art affects life. In *The Long Revolution* (1961), Williams wrote:

> If the art is part of the society, there is no solid whole, outside it, to which... we concede priority. The art is there, as an activity, with the production, the trading, the politics, the raising of families. To study the relations adequately we must study them actively, seeing all the activities as particular and contemporary forms of human energy.... It is then not a question of relating the art to the society, but of studying all the activities and their interrelations, without any concession of priority to any one of them we may choose to abstract.[9]

The first few sentences here put convincingly the case against one standard and reductionist Marxist model of base and superstructure. Williams emphasizes art as part of the social process. But the passage ends in a way that links Williams to Stephen. For while usefully rejecting the rigid model of base and superstructure, Williams yet postulates a kind of complexity in which, as in Stephen's earlier version, any sense of directing power or determination is absent. One studies "all the activities and their interrelations." It is true that, as he approaches his category "structure of feeling," Williams moves away, slightly, from this particular sense of complexity. "I would... define the theory of culture as the study of relationships between elements in a whole way of life. The analysis of culture is the attempt to discover the nature of the organization which is the complex of these relationships."[10] Now the complexity of relationships is seen as having an organization, a shape, and the effort of analysis is to define this

9. Raymond Williams, *The Long Revolution* (Harmondsworth: Penguin Books, 1965 [1961]), pp. 61-62.

10. Ibid., p. 63.

organization, in the whole way of life. It is to this inherent, characteristic, pervasive organization that Williams gives the name "structure of feeling."

Ten years after *The Long Revolution*, writing with direct reference to a Marxist schema, Williams put his concept in touch with a major development of method in Lucien Goldmann. Williams wrote that he had put forward the idea of a structure of feeling "to indicate certain common characteristics in a group of writers but also of others, in a particular historical situation."[11] And he found, reading Goldmann, that Goldmann was attempting to formulate a concept of structure to contain the relation of social and literary facts.

> The foundation of this approach is the belief that all human activity is an attempt to make a significant response to a particular objective situation. Who makes this response? According to Goldmann, neither the individual nor any abstract group, but individuals in real and collective social relations. The significant response is a particular view of the world: an organizing view. And it is just this element of organization that is, in literature, the significant social fact. A correspondence of content between a writer and his world is less significant than this correspondence of organization, of structure. A relation of content may be mere reflection, but a relation of structure . . . can show us the organizing principle by which a particular view of the world, and from that the coherence of the social group which maintains it, really operates in consciousness.[12]

Here the idea of structure of feeling emphasizes correspondences of *structure* as the expression of particular social groups. In *The Long Revolution* structure of feeling almost served as a synonym for culture; now Williams differentiates among classes or groups within the culture.

Williams refined his idea yet further, though not explicitly, in his essay "Base and Superstructure in Marxist Cultural

---

11. Raymond Williams, "Literature and Sociology: In Memory of Lucien Goldmann," *New Left Review*, no. 67 (May–June 1971), p. 12.

12. Ibid., pp. 12–13.

Theory,"[13] which he published in late 1973. Although he reiterated in that essay his long-term rejection of the base-superstructure model, he complained that Lukács's notion of totality is subject, under loose interpretation, to a formulation that withdraws "from the claim that there is any process of determination."[14] So that here, significantly, Williams himself withdraws from the position of *The Long Revolution*, which had denied any "concession of priority." The essential economic structure now assumes a central place in his views which it did not hold ten years before. The concept of an organizing principle thus also finds mooring in the determining processes.

But the effort of his essay is to suggest a less monolithic and epochal model than base-superstructure. He wants to allow at once for the old idea of structure of feeling, which falsely stressed a kind of unity in culture, and to differentiate among classes and experiences. To do so Williams proposes a model to include the idea of dominant, residual, and emergent cultural forms. He sees each historical period as necessarily permeated by a dominant culture that yet lives in a vital relation with what has been surpassed and with what is in the process of becoming.[15]

In my own use, I have tended to stress structure of feeling as it appears in Williams's most recent version, and as perti-

13. *New Left Review*, no. 82 (November–December 1973).
14. Ibid., p. 7.
15. In his *Marxism and Literature* (Oxford: Oxford University Press, 1977), Williams restates and further refines "determination" and "structure of feeling." Although I do not think anything strikingly new appears in this discussion, perhaps it is worth quoting the following passage explaining "structure of feeling":

> The term is difficult, but "feeling" is chosen to emphasize a distinction from more formal concepts of "world-view" or "ideology." It is not only that we must go beyond formally held and systematic beliefs, though of course we have always to include them. It is that we are concerned with meanings and values as they are actively lived and felt, and the relations between these and formal or systematic beliefs are in practice variable (including historically variable), over a range from formal assent with personal dissent to the more nuanced interaction between selected and interpreted beliefs and acted and justified experiences. [P. 132]

nent to particular classes or social groupings. The virtue, for my own purposes, of the concept of structure of feeling is that while it need not be, necessarily, *typical*, it yet strives to detail the form of fundamental attitudes based on concrete social experience. I believe that in this form the concept overcomes Stephen's uncertainty about how to locate literature in the whole life of the culture, within the totality of consciousness.

As the reader will discover, I bring a broad social development to bear on very few novels, mainly those of Jane Austen, Charlotte Brontë, and Charles Dickens (and even here I have been selective). They are the major novelists of the Industrial Revolution. The novels I discuss are, I believe, either typical or important of their kind. The same book could have been written about a great many more novels. Nevertheless, my aim has been to demonstrate that these particular novels register the fundamental transformation of England from an agrarian to an industrial nation—from custom to capital.

After pointing to some connections between the idea of "value" in political economy, social feeling, and the novel in Chapter 2, I trace in Chapter 3 different expressions of "value" in *Pride and Prejudice*, *Mansfield Park*, *Jane Eyre*, and *Hard Times*. Chiefly I concentrate on methods of characterization and technical justification of character in these novels and key economic notions of value—for example, the extent to which value is the creation of individual effort or labor versus, say, inheritance. In Chapter 4 I look at *Mansfield Park* and *Shirley* as historical novels, and discuss Austen's and Brontë's uses of historical materials. My concluding chapter speculates about correspondences between the novel and wider social responses to courtship, crime, and the crowd.

A concluding invocation of Leslie Stephen. He claimed for his small book that he did not aim at original judgments. "What I hope is," he wrote, "that by bringing familiar facts together I may be able to bring out the nature of the connection between them" (p. 19). I share Stephen's hope for my own work.

CHAPTER TWO

The Sources of Value

I

THE Hammonds opened their study *The Town Labourer* with this quotation from Macaulay:

> Our fields are cultivated with a skill unknown elsewhere, with a skill which has extracted rich harvests from moors and morasses. Our houses are filled with conveniences which the kings of former times might have envied. Our bridges, our canals, our roads, our modes of communication fill every stranger with wonder. Nowhere are manufactures carried to such perfection. Nowhere does man exercise such a dominion over matter.[1]

This revealing passage contains a "typical," mystifying grammatical shift. When Macaulay speaks of the concrete activity of transformation, he speaks abstractly, in the passive voice: "Our fields are cultivated. . . . Our houses are filled. . . ." No mention is made of any person who cultivates fields or fills houses with conveniences. The human agent is absent. But at the end of the paragraph, when the interpretation of the details is offered, his construction changes and for the first time a person appears: "Nowhere does man exercise

---

1. J. L. and Barbara Hammond, *The Town Labourer, 1795–1832* (London: Longmans, 1911), p. 15.

26

such a dominion over matter." Even this imperial metaphor excludes the actual activity of man with nature, the activity that results in Macaulay's wonders. Nevertheless, here, in conclusion, man is introduced, but he is introduced in such a way as to suggest a single society, a society in which every person exercises dominion. To his audience (he was speaking in the debates on the Reform Bill) "man" would have had a very clear meaning: it would have meant the bourgeoisie, since Macaulay intended, as the Hammonds say, to contrast "the standard of English government and the standard of English life."[2] The point of the passage, then, is that the bourgeoisie effected the transformation of England into a modern society.

Macaulay's elevation of one class into "man" and his account of a splendid new England in which marvels appeared without any transforming work are absolutely at odds with Marx's well-known account of these same changes. These two contrasting views illustrate a major divide in responses to the Industrial Revolution. Marx's characteristic departure depends on a shift from abstract and passive constructions—and ideas—to a more concrete and active grammar. For Marx the transformation of nature into useful objects is effected by the labor of men and women; in fact, for Marx people are defined by their labor: labor is our *"life activity, productive life* itself."[3] By "acting on the external world and changing it" people at once transform nature and themselves.[4] The root transformation, therefore, is the transformation of men into men and women into women: the most important product of human labor is human society.

Politically, Macaulay's passage was very clever, arguing for the enfranchisement of one class and the exclusion of another

2. Ibid.

3. Karl Marx, *The Economic and Philosophic Manuscripts of 1844*, ed. with an introduction by Dirk J. Struik, trans. Martin Milligan (New York: International Publishers, 1964), p. 113.

4. Karl Marx, *Capital* (3 vols.; New York: International Publishers, 1967), I, 177.

while deftly mystifying differences of class by means of the single term "man." And of course, as a eulogy of the middle class, Macaulay's account had a certain truth to it. But it is insofar as we see Macaulay in the act of writing the history of his own time, and consequently in the process of shaping and expressing fundamental attitudes, that his paragraph assumes its most profound significance. For he denies the laboring activity of transformation and the men and women who "worked" this transformation in a way characteristic of a whole class, a whole structure of feeling, and a whole body of writing.

The contrast between Macaulay and Marx forms part of an essential debate of the years of the Industrial Revolution: the debate about the sources of value. In this debate the structure of feeling Macaulay expresses achieved its most complete form. Initially centered in political economy, the debate had broad repercussions; the methods of the debate, its vocabulary, and its conclusions were common to a whole range of discourse. I wish here briefly to explore some connections between political economy and the novel.

II

Labor was the first price, the original purchase-money that was paid for all things. It was not by gold or by silver, but by labor, that all the wealth of the world was originally purchased.

—ADAM SMITH, *Wealth of Nations*

Labor alone ... never varying in its own value is alone the ultimate and real standard by which the value of all commodities can at all times and places be estimated and compared. It is their real price: money is their nominal price only.

—ADAM SMITH, *Wealth of Nations*

Manufacture ... denotes every extensive product of art, which is made by machinery, with little or no aid of the human hand;

so that the most perfect manufacture is that which dispenses
entirely with manual labor.[5]
—ANDREW URE, *The Philosophy of Manufactures*

Each of these passages has its place in the history of economic
thought; but I am interested in them rather as statements in a
kind of social autobiography, as critical efforts to interpret and
define a developing social transformation. It is clear, I think,
that a merely technical reading of these passages is just not
possible. Adam Smith, for instance, tried to distinguish between the nominal and the real. The distinction is obviously
important in the terms of political economy alone, for as the
society rapidly moved into the age of industrial capitalism, the
basis of value had to be established with some theoretical integrity. But the process of transformation that Smith saw as
economic of course was reverberating through the whole society; not only were the means of production being transformed, but so were essential social relationships. Not only
was Smith concerned to distinguish between the nominal and
the real, but so was Jane Austen.

Smith was brought to this distinction because he wanted to
find both the *source* of value and the stable "real standard" of

5. Cf. Kenneth Burke, *A Grammar of Motives and a Rhetoric of Motives*
(New York: World, 1962), p. 109:
   Since technology, as the primary characterizing feature of our second
   nature today, is "substantially" human, in accordance with the
   paradox of substance it can become quite "inhuman." For while the
   accumulations of the industrial plant are "in principle" the externalization or alienation of intrinsically human virtues, there are many
   unintended by-products. . . . For this externalization of internal ap-
   titudes is different in its state of *being* than in its *becoming*. It is in its
   becoming that technology most fully represents the human agent. . . .
   In its state of *being* . . . it can change from a *purpose* into a *problem*. And
   surely much of the anguish of the modern world derives from the
   paradoxical fact that machinery, as the embodiment of rationality in
   its most rational moments, has in effect translated rationality itself
   from the realm of ideal aims to the realm of material requirements.
   Few ironies are richer in complexities than the irony of man's servitude to his mechanical servants.

value in a world in which they were already obscured by the profusion of commodities. That is, the *new* system of commodities was with him, as it were, and he saw and experienced it everywhere. To find the value, the essential value, of commodities, he needed to look into them and into their origins. To do so Smith, in a manner Ruskin, among others, later followed, posited a model of original relationships, his classic picture of a hunting nation in which a deer and a beaver are "exchanged." This model portrayed, as the economist Joan Robinson says, an "idyllic past" in which the laborer got back the full value of his labor without landlord or factory owner to taint moral relationships.[6] Nonetheless in this original model Smith made a vital discovery for the history of political economy: that labor is at once the source and creator of value and the standard of value.

In the autobiography of industrial capitalism, the notion that labor creates value was at once liberating and dangerous; but in either case it marked a definitive break with other notions of the source of value, especially those based on inheritance and tradition. If labor is the source of value, then social life and its products and the meaning of social life all derive from human activity. It is not accidental that in Marx the labor theory of value and Hegel's historicism unite to formulate a finally whole account of capitalist development. But the point for the history and understanding of the English novel is that this discovery is neither continental nor *ex post* but inherent in the fundamental attitudes of England's most developed interpretation of the Industrial Revolution.

A further aspect of Smith's account of value bears importantly on the novel. Smith tried to establish the real value of things in a society in which the medium of transactions and thus of economic judgment was money. He wanted to look behind money at the real meaning of transactions. Yet even as he outlined his original model to explain real value, Smith

6. Joan Robinson, *Economic Philosophy* (Chicago: Aldine, 1962), p. 29.

spoke in the language of the extant, dominant, moneyed system. Labor is the "purchase-money that was paid for all things." Value, the real standard by which things are judged, is their "price." Smith's whole mode of thought was permeated by what Ruskin later called mercantile language. This is true to such an extent that Smith was most deeply drawn to the essential terms of the moneyed system at the very point where he wanted to throw it off and speak of an earlier, pristine economic condition. So that although Smith perceived labor as the source of value, it was difficult for him fully to realize the implications of this perception, because he could not, at heart, think in any terms but those of sales, prices, purchases, and gold. The imaginative presence of primitive exchange was far weaker in his account than the volatile, complete presence of what he yet called nominal value.

Here, in the novel, is an instance of a similar difficulty:

> It is a truth universally acknowledged, that a single man in possession of a good fortune must be in want of a wife.
> However little known the feelings or views of such a man may be on his first entering a neighborhood, this truth is so well fixed in the minds of the surrounding families, that he is considered as the rightful property of some one or other of their daughters.[7]

This opening has received much attention. The passage is humorously ironic; it seeks to distinguish between nominal value, which is overt fortune, and real value, which resides in feeling and character. The passage mocks the attitude of the neighborhood, and yet to do so it employs the very mercantile language it wishes to disavow: the man who is in "possession" of a good fortune becomes in turn the "property" of an available daughter. The passage turns on the meanings of a word it doesn't use: "worth." And in doing so it displays a "typical" tension between the surface argument, in which truths are spoken of as "fixed," and the sense of as yet unformed and

7. *Pride and Prejudice*, in *The Novels of Jane Austen*, ed. R. W. Chapman (5 vols.; 3d ed.; London: Oxford University Press, 1966 [1923]), II, 1.

very fluid relationships, responses, and feelings implicit below the surface. As the chapter continues, and then as the novel enters fully into its action, the fine distinction between nominal and real value threatens to disappear in a perplexing but perhaps dynamic resolution (though not a synthesis) of opposites. For what becomes dramatized is the maxim of the opening sentence, no longer from the distance of criticism and irony but simply as enactment. When we return to the opening sentences after Darcy has married Elizabeth, we are far less likely to take them as jest. The fluidity below the surface of the first few paragraphs becomes, by the novel's end, surprisingly fixed. We can see as well that here, as in Smith, the vital concern to distinguish between nominal and real value is complicated by the unsettling truth that the very language of distance, irony, and judgment is itself shot through with the fundamental attitudes of moneyed society.

In turning to Andrew Ure, we find a different set of problems. Smith published in 1776, Ure in 1835; Smith tried to uncover the reality of a system, Ure became its apologist; Smith wrote, in a sense, to facilitate the triumph of industrial capitalism, Ure wrote to maintain its hegemony. England had been transformed by 1835, and Ure announced one consequence of this transformation in consciousness. For Smith labor was the source of value: his mode was optimistic in the revolutionary sense that it argued for the ability of human beings to shape social life. For Ure the nature of progress became suddenly mystical: "the most perfect manufacture is that which dispenses entirely with manual labour." One rummages in this sentence, with its ethically base use of "perfect" and its revealing, imperial "dispenses," for the source of value. If perfection is the absence of labor, of what is it the presence? Machinery, Ure appears to say; but are not machines also made? The change from 1776 to 1835, then, is a change between definition and description on the one hand and mystification on the other. That this mystification is integral to Ure's role as an apologist for a now ascendant system becomes immediately clear when we follow him from his dismissal of labor to his dismissal of laborers:

> Arkwright alone had the sagacity to discern... how vastly productive human industry would become, when no longer proportioned in its results to muscular effort, which by its nature is fitful and capricious, but when made to consist in the task of guiding the work of mechanical fingers and arms, regularly impelled with great velocity by some indefatigable physical power. [The main difficulty in realizing this vision lay] in training human beings to renounce their desultory habits of work, and to identify themselves with the unvarying regularity of the complex automaton.[8]

Elsewhere, writing of the invention of the self-acting mule, Ure says:

> He [the commissioned machinist] produced... a machine apparently instinct with the thought, feeling, and tact of the experienced workman.... Thus, the *Iron Man* [Ure's italics], as the operatives fitly call it, sprung out of the hands of our modern Prometheus at the bidding of Minerva—a creation destined to restore order among the industrious classes, and to confirm to Great Britain the empire of art. [P. 367]

For us "art" and "industry" have been sundered; Ure wrote at the very point when the cleavage occurred, when "art" had virtually lost its older meaning as "skill" and had come into its modern usage in association with culture and aesthetics; and when "industry" had also moved away from its meaning as "skill," but in an opposite direction.[9] By 1835 art and culture had become terms used, within an increasingly coherent structure of feeling, to mount a vital attack on industrial capitalism. Ure's insistence on the untransformed meanings forms part of his argument against those who, like Hazlitt and Cobbett early

8. Andrew Ure, *The Philosophy of Manufactures: Or, An Exposition of the Scientific, Moral, and Commercial Economy of the Factory System of Great Britain* (London: Charles Knight, 1835), pp. 14–15. Further references are cited in the text.

9. See the discussion of these words in Raymond Williams, *Keywords* (New York: Oxford University Press, 1976).

in the century and Ruskin later, rose in outrage, and in the name of art and culture, against the proposition that progress means the transformation of the worker into a machine and the machine into a human being. This perverse transformation is the dark shadow of Marx's progressive account. In Ure the worker must "identify himself with . . . the complex automaton" while the machine develops fingers, arms, thought, feeling, tact, and becomes an Iron Man! Smith's ethical concern to distinguish nominal from real vanishes in Ure behind a grossly inappropriate classical allusion; Ure blithely unravels his vision of a progress devoid of working men and women, an empire peopled by self-acting automatons.

When Ure published *Philosophy of Manufactures* in 1835, Britain had not yet fully emancipated its slaves; this process was not completed until around 1840. Moreover, the lives of many of its people were passed in labor in the fields, in service, and in labor in the factories. It was *this* society that embraced and gloried in Ure's notion of progress without workers. As the new class of industrial capitalists became ideologically more assertive—as for instance in effecting passage of the brutal new Poor Law—the question of the source of value became at once more complex and more explosive. By the 1830s the idea that labor creates value carried with it obviously dangerous implications.[10] An index of the rising system of feeling was the transference of the human names of the laborers—slave, servant, and man—to the machine. The machine is seen as a slave or servant in a society one segment of which is increasingly eager to obfuscate both its own origins and the sources of wealth—whether they be in "trade" and thus not adequately genteel or in labor and thus socially and politically threatening; and which, in its increasing complacency, is content to think of labor in terms of slaves and servants. In this society the attitude of those in power toward laboring was that "our" slaves, our servants, our "men" would

10. See Robinson, *Economic Philosophy* , p. 34.

do it for "us." It was a short step to "Our money will work for use" or "Our self-acting machines will work for us." These mystifications confuse Smith's idea of the source of value in a fashion of great relevance to literature. If wealth is the outcome not of labor, effort, or activity, but gets created, as it were, by magic, then cannot all value be gained in the same way? Is not civilization, our civilized life, also precisely this kind of spontaneous creation? And is not what is truly valuable utterly detached from, separate from, and superior to "material" life? In short, are not money and morals, function and character, life and art distinct and autonomous realms of meaning and being?

The industrialist of 1776 was intent on transforming the conditions of his and his nation's life. In 1835 a different emphasis emerges as power comes into range. If money appears from a bank, in a wonderful way, increasing and multiplying as if by the medium of a wonderful spell; and if money also translates into whatever one may want, also as it were by magic, then the very existence of social relationships can be ignored. The human relationship between landlord and laborer or between owner and worker gets pushed out of sight; and the wealth produced by labor similarly becomes invisible. But to the laborer in field or factory it will have been perfectly clear that work is done by men and women and not by money or machinery. Privileged versions of the sources of value— such as Ure's—were therefore fiercely contested.

No one contested them more than William Cobbett. Here he writes of his hated national debt and taxation, which, he maintains, have

> a natural tendency to *draw wealth into great masses*. These masses produce a power of *congregating* manufacturers, and of making the many work at them, *for the gain of a few*.... The land suffers greatly from this.... The country people lose part of their natural employment... the Lords of the Loom have now a set of *real* slaves, by the means of whom they take away a great part of the employment of the country-*women* and *girls*....

To counter the Lords of the Loom, Cobbett proposes his own *"straw affair,"* to

> restore to the land some of the employment of its women and girls. It will be impossible for... any of the horse-power or steam-power or air-power ruffians... to draw together bands of men, women, and children, and to make them slaves, in the working of *straw*. The raw material comes *of itself*; and the *hand*, and the *hand alone*, can convert it to use.... If I had not been *certain*, that... no *white slave* holder, could ever arise out of it, assuredly one line upon the subject never would have been written by me. Better, a million times, that the money... should go to enrich even the rivals and enemies of the country; than that it should enable these hard, these unfeeling men, to draw English people into crowds and make them slaves, and slaves too of the lowest and most degraded cast.[11]

Cobbett wrote these words well before he was elected, after the Reform Act, as M.P. for Oldham; but he wrote here against the conventions that sharply differentiated city from country. The relation between the Lords of the Loom and the life of the countryside is obvious and assumed, and the absence of any self-consciousness about the connection illustrates the breadth of the crisis in consciousness. The differences between one and another account of the source of value are shown to involve the whole life of the nation. Moreover, in this passage, as in Ure's, the clash of opinion is also a clash of words themselves, a conflict over usage and meaning. The Lords of the Loom have not merely a set of mechanical slaves but of *real* slaves; the Lords of the Loom are *white slave* holders. Cobbett rises up against the confusion of the real meaning of the word "slave" by its transference to a machine, crying out rightly that the actual transformation is of black slaves into white.[12] In the hands of the Lords of the Loom the

---

11. William Cobbett, *Rural Rides*, ed. George Woodcock (Harmondsworth: Penguin Books, 1967 [first published 1830]), pp. 117–18. Cobbett's italics.

12. Cf. Engels: "The bourgeoisie has gained a monopoly of all means of existence in the broadest sense of the word. What the proletarian needs, he

machine *enslaves:* thus Cobbett anticipates Ure and responds to him. And Cobbett's proposal for the production of straw goods, by hand, offers at once a real alternative mode of production and a critique of mercantile language. Cobbett would not have men and women reduced to mere hands, as in the usage of the Lords of the Loom, but would rather they live decently by means of handwork.

In *Rural Rides*, upon reaching Burghclere a number of days after having left Reigate, Cobbett traces his path back, listing estate by estate the disappearance of the old landowners, with their old names, their lineage, and their supposedly humane moral economy, and then the new owners, tradesmen, bankers, West Indians, the purveyors of the new moneyed system. Certainly, as my own sentence perhaps suggests, Cobbett sweetens the vision of an older England in unfair contrast with what has come; he ignores the exploitive nature of the old system and the arbitrary power of the old landlords and clergy; he ignores the gradual erosion of the old system of rights over a century or more, and ignores the gradual but definite capitalization of the countryside over the same span of years; and having done so, he focuses the accumulated change of a century into his current list, after the Napoleonic wars, of changes in ownership.[13] Obviously it is inaccurate to say, as Cobbett did, that bankers and West Indians suddenly came upon English life in the 1820s, or for that matter in the 1790s. Nevertheless I believe that Cobbett did accurately portray the *felt* change; as he watched, changes in daily life accumulated into an explosive force, and he gave to the reaction of a vast portion of the population a representative voice. However tenuous the real community that Cobbett saw passing away

---

can obtain only from this bourgeoisie, which is protected in its monopoly by the power of the State. The proletarian is, therefore, in law and in fact, the slave of the bourgeoisie, which can decree his life or his death" (*Condition of the Working Class in England* [London: Panther, 1969], p. 109).

13. Cobbett, *Rural Rides*, pp. 269–70.

may have been, he recorded its breakdown in a fashion of great importance for his own time and for English culture: he defined what was happening as a clash between two whole systems, two wholly different social expressions of value. It is from his standpoint within the older moral economy that Cobbett resists the devaluations of relationship and meaning which he identifies with the system of the Lords of the Loom. Even when Cobbett's general judgments are wrong—and they are not, after all, very often wrong—and even when he is simply making up a vision of the past, the very concreteness of Cobbett's account—this straw affair against that mill—offers actual instances of comparison that illuminate the conflict over the source of value *in the present*. Of course we know, since Cobbett tells us plainly, that his touchstone of value is the condition of the laborer. And so we know too what Cobbett's notion of value will mean for the actual life of actual people. In Ure not only is the source of value mystified, but the implications of his system for people's lives remain ominously unstated. We are left to draw our conclusions—which are usually unpleasant enough.

III

Cobbett and Ure judge differently what makes for life; but as well, in the contrast of their judgments, the question of *whose* life is paramount. Cobbett's notation of the impact of the industrial system on the life of the countryside puts emphasis on the central historical development; Ure's enthusiasm for self-reproducing machines, while important as an index of consciousness, serves us badly if we want to know what actually took place. During the Industrial Revolution the novel, like almost everything else, located itself in the country. Cobbett is helpful, therefore, although the novels also display the lives of people he doesn't say much about: women. As we conclude this initial discussion of value it is crucial therefore to turn to developments in the countryside as they affected the lives of women.

Sheila Rowbotham draws attention to the changing architecture of the farmhouse. She notes that, as capitalism transformed the countryside, the great kitchen in which the farmer and his laborers ate together gave way to a small dining room for the farmer and his family and a devalued kitchen for the help. This new room appeared at the same time as another in the increasingly important big houses of prosperous farmers—the bedroom.[14] A whole history at a point of determining transition can be read in the appearance of these two small rooms.

First, this is the history of the differentiation among classes in the countryside.

> The well-to-do, landowner and farmer alike, grew richer and changed their way of living, because they were able to make it more comfortable and to their taste; the less well-to-do became poorer and changed their way of living because they had to. The stratification of society according to a new system went on apace, and the several income grades of women in rural society, like their husbands, drew steadily away from one another because the disparity of their incomes caused such wide divergences in behavior, outlook, and environment.[15]

The disparity of incomes was not just a question of money but of kinds of work done, kinds of households managed, and kinds of activities pursued for learning and diversion. Some farmers and landowners could, eventually, afford a visit to London; and the wealthy went to visit London annually. To the difference of income was added the increasingly defining difference of culture.

As "behavior, outlook, and environment" diverged, one class increasingly became invisible to the other, or at best put out of mind. The laborers, once intimate with their employers, now suffered a kind of exile into their own narrowed

14. Sheila Rowbotham, *Hidden from History* (New York: Vintage Books, 1976), pp. 23, 3.
15. G. E. and K. R. Fussell, *The English Countrywoman: A Farmhouse Social History*, A.D. *1500–1900* (New York: Benjamin Blom, 1971 [1953]), p. 156.

community; familiarity gave way to distance. The active creation of wealth by laborers, indeed their whole social presence in the rural economy, became submerged within the picturesqueness of the country seat and its adorning, and equally picturesque, villages. The Fussells quote the account of Mary Cox, 35, a laborer; she describes her life early in the nineteenth century in what they name as a famous "picturesque village," Milton Abbas in Dorset:

> "When I was about seventeen I lived with my father and mother, two sisters older than I was and a brother fourteen years old in a cottage at Milton Abbas. Robert Vacher and his wife with three children, about one, two, and three years old, lived in the same cottage. We had the two rooms downstairs, and the Vachers the two upstairs. There were only four rooms in the cottage. There were two cottages in the building. My father and mother, two sisters and young brother slept in the back room downstairs.... The Vachers still live in the same two rooms, and they have six children living with them.... The cottages in Milton Abbas are very crowded ... they sometimes put up a curtain between the beds. I believe there are a great many bastards in Milton Abbas."[16]

One gauges here a definitive social distance. In Mary Cox's home a very different architecture prevails from that of the home of a prosperous yeoman, not to say a landowner. We find neither a new bedroom nor a new dining room but two crowded all-purpose rooms, with perhaps some curtains between the several beds. Mary Cox pays witness to the sexual consequences of these arrangements. The Fussells also quote on this subject the diary of the Reverend B. J. Armstrong of East Dereham, Norfolk: "'I find cleanliness on the increase in the parish, but no diminution of illegitimacy. The girls see nothing sinful in it, and their mothers, apparently, connive at it.'"[17] Ignoring the Reverend Armstrong's gratuitous remark about the mothers, we face, in his remarks and those of Mary

16. Ibid., pp. 176–77.
17. Ibid., p. 174.

Cox, the startling fact that during the years of the Industrial Revolution there occurred throughout Europe a phenomenal rise in working-class illegitimacy. The rise in illegitimacy is a signal of a complex process of readjustment of personal life, especially of the lives of women, during the transition to industrial capitalism. The complexity of the process can be seen in the disconcertingly various impact of similar conditions on the farmers, laborers, and landowners.

The increase of illegitimacy has been attributed primarily to the rise of sexual intercourse before marriage, which has been named the "central fact in the history of courtship over the last two centuries."[18] But although there seems to be considerable evidence of a generally nonrepressive sexual atmosphere among all classes of English society in the latter half of the eighteenth century, the rise in illegitimacy occurred within the lower classes. More important is the larger trend of which illegitimacy is one part: toward a central emphasis on emotional compatibility and then romantic love in marriage.[19] These developments raise the question of value in a new way.

18. Edward Shorter, *The Making of the Modern Family* (New York: Basic Books, 1975), p. 80.
19. Ibid., p. 148. According to Lawrence Stone, *The Family, Sex, and Marriage in England, 1500-1800* (Harmondsworth: Penguin Books, 1979 [abr. and rev. ed.]), "the rising rates of pre-marital pregnancy and illegitimacy affected the peasantry, the artisans, and the poor in the late eighteenth century, but not the upper middle class, the gentry, and the aristocracy" (p. 23). He also writes:

By 1660 ... it had been conceded, in the interests of "holy matrimony," that children of both sexes should be given the right of veto over a future spouse proposed to them by their parents. Between 1660 and 1800, however, there took place a far more radical shift ... with the children now normally making their own choices, and the parents being left with no more than the right of veto over socially or economically unsuitable candidates. At the same time there was inevitably a marked shift of emphasis on motives away from family interest and towards well-tried personal affection. Almost everyone agreed, however, that both physical desire and romantic love were unsafe bases for an enduring marriage, since both were violent mental disturbances which would inevitably be of only short duration. [P. 183]

Although the point at issue is still, What are the sources of value?, the arena of meaning is not economic life in its "public" sense but, now, the "determined" private life of love, courtship, and marriage.

In speaking of the appearance of private bedrooms in the houses of yeomen, Sheila Rowbotham sees the emergence of "a stable monogamous home unit appropriate to capitalism."[20] Mary Cox's life in Milton Abbas did not induce the value of monogamy but the very opposite. Illegitimacy can be seen as the expression of a social network in which either familial stability is unimportant or the communal restrictions and repressions that ensure family solidity have broken down. The history of the modern family suggests that both possibilities obtained. The capitalization of the countryside and the transformation of the older rituals of the country into the self-seeking of rural capitalism, especially during the years of industrialization, loosened the communal and customary morality in private relations as well as in the political economy. The hold of the community weakened at the same time that the passions of the self were given legitimacy. The restraints against illegitimacy loosened at the same time that individual choice in courtship and individual passion in relationships were set free.[21]

But, as the Fussells note, this is also a countryside in the process of stratification. The laborer was drawn into wage work and competition, but so was the small farmer. It was the successful small farmer who built himself a bedroom; it was the successful small farmer who wanted to stabilize his holdings, increase his income, maintain a tight family unit through which property could be consolidated and passed on. But it was precisely the small farmer grown to independent status under capitalism who, by building himself a bedroom, signaled a change in the valuation of romance in marriage. His

20. Rowbotham, *Hidden from History*, p. 3.
21. Shorter, *Making of the Modern Family*, pp. 251-61.

marriage was no longer a communal ritual that retained a kind
of public character, the wife taking one bed with him among
several and one chair at a large, communal table. The thrust of
the market, which stressed individual value, pushed the customary arrangements under and brought up a new sense of
private sexual compatibility. Perhaps here also we discover a
conflict between men and women. The woman, previously
ignored as a person in the marriage arrangements, becomes, as
she assumes the new awareness of self, insistent on some mode
of fulfillment in her central life event, marriage. This becomes
even more true of women in the capacity of wage earners, who
can now make sexual arrangements out of a new sense of
power. It is perfectly sensible that it should have been Mary
Wollstonecraft, one of a new breed of women writers actually
living off their earnings, who wrote the feminist manifesto of
the Industrial Revolution.

The situation of the prosperous small farmer was roughly
equivalent to the situation of the lesser gentry, the people we
meet in the novels of Jane Austen and later of Charlotte
Brontë. In Austen's and Brontë's worlds the possibilities and
dangers of fortune among the lesser gentry are amply displayed. You can move up but you can fall; your income
may increase but you may fall into ruin—a prospect that
threatens the Bennets after the father's death. Estates may be
enlarged but also endangered or even lost, as in *Mansfield Park*
and *Persuasion*. People of this class thus find themselves in a
pivotal position: the pressure of rural capitalism forces them to
compete for their survival, draws them into the economy of
money and landed capital, and thereby creates, in a sharper
way even than for the farmers, a crisis in consciousness. One
reaction to this pressure will be to stabilize, maintain value,
marry for money, improve the land; another will be to differentiate oneself, to seek one's individuality, to maintain family against community. Yet community, as the old way of life,
also exerts its pressure. These possible pressures and responses are focused especially on courtship and marriage for

the women of this class. Partly the process looks like this:

> The big, in order to save themselves from being *"swallowed up quick"*..., make use of their *voices* to get, through place, pension, or sinecure, something back from the taxers. Others of them *fall in love* with the *daughters* and *widows* of paper-money people, big brewers, and the like; and sometimes their daughters *fall in love* with the paper-money people's sons, or the fathers of those sons.[22]

Thus Cobbett. One cannot say he does not describe actual events, actual marriages, the arrangements that were actually made. Yet even Cobbett here employs, in mockery, the language of romance: "their daughters *fall in love* with the paper-money people's sons." But what do the daughters and sons think and feel as they fall in love? The conflict of their emotions is exemplified in the novels of Jane Austen and Charlotte Brontë. And in these novels this transformation assumes shape, in consciousness, around the question of value in courtship and marriage.

IV

If the writings of Macaulay and Marx may be called a form of social autobiography, this is obviously and explicitly true of the novel. I mean by social autobiography the effort in consciousness to interpret, to define, and then to affect the developing social transformation. The accounts of Macaulay and Marx—and those of Smith, Ure, and Cobbett—provide different standards of value by which to understand, to judge, and consequently to direct those developments. In the novel of these years the question of value usually is raised within court-

---

22. Cobbett, *Rural Rides*, p. 27; his italics. Cf. Mary Wollstonecraft: "Girls marry to better themselves, to borrow a significant vulgar phrase, and have such perfect power over their hearts as not to permit themselves to fall in love till a man with superior fortune offers" (Wollstonecraft, *The Rights of Woman*, and John Stuart Mill, *The Subjection of Women* [London: J. M. Dent, 1965], p. 83).

ship. Courtship exemplifies the nature of change by forcing the question of self. Am I worthy of him? Is he worthy of me? Here, in the two meanings of "worth," is one crucial connection between political economy and literature. Does worth mean cash, land, talent? Is there a nominal and a true meaning of the word? Are individuals the creators of their own worth?

Cobbett shows that a particular notion of value implies a particular system of human relationships. Partly the novel confronts social transformation directly in terms of the system of relationships, in terms of class. But most deeply the novel investigates the sources of value in the self: can we make our own characters and our own lives or are we passively the products of family, community, or nation? Or does character emerge out of some process of interaction?

CHAPTER THREE

The Production of Value: Education, Activity, and Character

I

THE novels of Jane Austen, Charlotte Brontë, and Charles Dickens narrate the coming of age of children and young adults. They focus on the new generation, which is consciously seen as new, as different from the older generation and on the brink of a significantly new life. What happens to the children is a sign of the author's judgment of his or her society, and often this judgment is overtly aimed at a novel's main responsible, which is to say adult, figure, usually the father but frequently the mother or aunt or guardian. The older generation exemplifies the society. It is at once responsible for the reproduction and maintenance of social relationships, of social value, and serves the children as the concrete instance of what is to come. The children must shrewdly assess the life of the older generation as they enter on their

I am using the following editions, which I will refer to by chapter and page number in the text; when a novel is printed in volumes, I will give the volume citation as well: *The Novels of Jane Austen*, ed. R. W. Chapman (5 vols.; 3d ed.; London: Oxford University Press, 1966 [1923]); Charlotte Brontë, *Jane Eyre*, ed. Margaret Smith (London: Oxford University Press, 1973); *The Works of Charles Dickens* (40 vols.; National ed.; London: Chapman & Hall, 1906–1908).

own; but, because in these novels change has, in varying degrees, overtaken fixed routines, the children cannot altogether—sometimes not at all—rely on the adults. Often the adults have failed to maintain a vital social life and the children must somehow salvage a damaged structure.

Obviously these patterns are not accidental or merely structures of fiction. They express, by means of a socially compelling set of concepts—the growth of the child, the fortunes of the family, the courtship of sons and daughters—the observed histories of people within the emergent society. The process of transformation not only created "a stable monogamous home unit" but, because of the sudden acceleration of tempo, the new leap from decade to decade, also established an unprecedented break between the generations. The children are no longer distinguished from the adults simply by age; the children are no longer, that is, defined only by their immaturity. Although, of course, immaturity and lack of self-knowledge and of knowledge of the world remain crucial and central, the new fact is that the children in some ways have access to a universe of experience basically different from that of their parents; and therefore, the children are at once immature and yet possessed of a knowledge the adults do not have. The process of transformation shapes the generations differently, forming the adults by one complex of events and the children by another. In Jane Austen's novels, where the adult generation receives its fullest homage, the separation between the courting couples and the married ones could not, on the whole, be sharper. By the time we come to Dickens, of course, the separation has become extreme.

Under these circumstances in the society and in the fiction, the novelist is pressed to ask: What are the sources of real value in this changing society? How can value be effectively produced (or reproduced)—that is, what sort of education will create "good" people? Has the older generation met its responsibility for educating the younger? These questions of theme and ideology are intimately bound with a parallel aesthetic question: How will a fictional character be "justified," be shown to have become such and such a person?

In Thomas Day's tremendously popular *History of Sandford and Merton* (1783–89), Tommy Merton's tutor, Mr. Barlow, establishes one kind of answer to these questions. His starting point, as he tours the countryside with his pupil and comments on it, is Adam Smith's account of value: "Without labor, these fertile fields which are now adorned with all the luxuriance of plenty would be converted into barbarous heaths... these meadows... be covered with stagnated waters...."[1] The implicit association here between value and improvement is eventually made explicit; for the moment Mr. Barlow draws his anti-aristocratic lesson: "for this reason... labor is the first and most indispensable duty of the human species." The idle aristocrats in their manors are in this way maligned and exposed, leading Tommy, at the end of his education, to affirm that "all men [are] his brethren and equals" and to conclude, appropriately: "I now plainly perceive that a man may be of much more consequence by improving his mind in various kinds of knowledge, than by all the finery and magnificence he can acquire."

So here, the method and structure of political economy are reproduced in educational theory. Of course the debates about education involved matters of curriculum and instruction; but centrally, and of course on the whole in the novel, the main concern remained this one with moral training. And the way Smith's notion of value was put to use is accurately assessed by the educational historian Brian Simon; he says, in his comments on *Sandford and Merton*, that its focus on certain kinds of moral training implied "a belief that education can change men's nature."[2]

---

1. This is Brian Simon's observation in his definitive *The Two Nations and the Educational Structure, 1780–1870* (London: Lawrence & Wishart, 1974) [first published 1960 as *Studies in the History of Education, 1780–1870*], p. 41. The quotations from *Sandford and Merton* are from vol. 2, pp. 268–69; vol. 3, p. 298; and vol. 3, p. 255, which Simon quotes on pp. 41–42.

2. Simon, *Two Nations*, p. 44.

This idea—that education can change men's nature—finds expression in the writing of many progressive or radical thinkers. It can be traced to David Hartley's *Observations on Man* (1749) and to the tendencies of associational psychology in general; to such publications as the Edgeworths' influential *Practical Education* (1798); and to William Godwin's *Enquiry Concerning Political Justice* (1793), with its argument that nothing stands between the individual and his or her full flowering but the exertion of individual effort. This point of view, then, reflects the vigorous middle class of eighteenth-century England and Scotland and its enterprising, energetic, often radical scientific and political figures.[3]

In the novel, partly Tommy Merton's progressive conclusion is simply accepted; partly the structure of the individual's quest from childhood to maturity and success necessarily stresses Merton's point of view. One stream of meaning, then, maintains that the individual can significantly shape his or her life. But sometimes, even alongside this first position, another conservative one gets put, roughly after Burke in its view that "human nature" is fixed and that value is a precious inheritance from the past rather than something human activity creates in each generation. Finally, one also finds a position in the manner of Macaulay and Ure, in which the source of value, the justification of character, remains utterly obscure, is in fact mystified, and character is simply asserted as a given.

II

The elder Mr. Darcy and his wife are dead before the action of *Pride and Prejudice* begins, but we hear them (especially Mr. Darcy) spoken of in tones of general and unrestrained admiration. The Bennets, however, we see up close and know very well at firsthand. Darcy's home and the shaping circumstances of his life are hidden for a good part of the book—we know more about his money than about his land, and we see him as

3. Ibid., pp. 45–46.

an autonomous agent rather than as a person bound to his defining environment. This initial portrait of Darcy is part of Jane Austen's plan: it allows us later to "reread" him, to share in Elizabeth's change of heart, and consequently to assent to it. But because Darcy's full social context remains for so long, and in some respects altogether, unsketched, we may not observe as forcefully as we ought that the senior Darcy, like Mr. Bennet, has miseducated his children, and that the Darcy home, like the Bennet home, is seriously flawed. Near the end of the novel Darcy himself explains this to us:

> "As a child, I was taught what was *right;* but I was not taught to correct my temper. I was given good principles, but left to follow them in pride and conceit. Unfortunately, an only son (so many years an only *child*), I was spoilt by my parents, who, though good themselves (my father particularly, all that was benevolent and amiable), allowed, encouraged, almost taught me to be selfish and overbearing—to care for none beyond my own family circle, to think meanly of all the rest of the world, to *wish* at least to think meanly of their sense and worth compared with my own. . . . and such I might still have been but for you, dearest, loveliest Elizabeth! . . . You taught me a lesson, hard indeed at first, but most advantageous." [III, chap. 16, 369]

Of Darcy's "family circle" Jane Austen allows us to meet his cousin Colonel Fitzwilliam, Darcy's sister Georgiana, and, chiefly, his aunt Lady Catherine de Bourgh and her sickly daughter, ostensibly affianced to Darcy in her cradle. Georgiana, the slightest of the important characters in the novel, seems, as the saying goes, very nice, but we do not really think much about her. Colonel Fitzwilliam, of more substance, may be engaging yet also plays a minor role; nonetheless, he salvages Darcy's "family circle" from what would necessarily be a very bad opinion, since the formidable representative of that group in the novel is the base Lady Catherine. The frail Miss de Bourgh, counterpoint to Elizabeth, serves to point up the weakness of Darcy's aristocratic side, its symbolic decline. There is, it is true, no indication in the novel that Darcy ever intended to marry Lady Catherine's daughter; but the failure of his parents, absent though they are, is that they educated him for this narrow society only, a narrow society the most visible representatives of which exemplify a life at once reprehensible and utterly enfeebled. By the end of the novel, then, we have a clear sense of the forces that shaped Darcy's personality and of the perils to which this education exposed him. We will not, in this light, think Darcy is being merely gallant in saying that Elizabeth "taught [him] a lesson, hard . . . but most advantageous."[4]

Does the educational metaphor imply that Elizabeth's "lesson" changed Darcy's nature? The novel clearly argues that character is "made": this is the ground for the criticism of Mr. Bennet. When Lydia pleads to be allowed exposure at Brighton, Mr. Bennet permits it, tempering his irresponsibility with wit in protesting to Elizabeth that Lydia will never be satisfied without a proper fling at folly, and " 'we can never expect her to do it with so little expense or inconvenience to her family' " (II, chap. 18, 230). But the Elizabeth who hears these words is already growing into the woman who will command Pemberley, and her former tolerance of wit at the expense of irresponsibility now reverses itself:

> Elizabeth . . . had never been blind to the impropriety of her father's behavior as a husband. . . . She [had] endeavoured . . . to banish from her thoughts that continual breach of conjugal obligation and decorum which, in exposing his wife to the contempt of his own children, was so highly reprehensible. But she had never . . . been so fully aware of the evils arising from so ill-judged a direction of talents; talents which, rightly used, might at least have preserved the respectability of his daughters, even if incapable of enlarging the mind of his wife. [II, chap. 19, 236–37]

4. Cf. Harrison R. Steeves, *Before Jane Austen: The Shaping of the English Novel in the Eighteenth Century* (New York: Holt, Rinehart & Winston, 1965), p. 347: "This is the first time in a major fiction that a conflict of emotional interests involves criticism of the aristocrat not on the familiar ground of the traditional vices of his class, but for the injury that birth and breeding have done to this personality."

Elizabeth's journey in *Pride and Prejudice* is away from irony; her new awareness is a main signal of her steps along that journey. The "spirit of activity" that Mrs. Norris displays in *Mansfield Park* (*MP*, I, chap. 1, 4) here propels Mrs. Bennet, and the charge laid against *Mr.* Bennet is that by *inactivity* he has abandoned his daughters to their fates, that he has withdrawn from his responsibility to shape their natures by active instruction. The seriousness of the charge is aggravated by the family's extremely tenuous hold on gentility. During Mr. Bennet's lifetime the family enjoys a reasonably affluent income, £2,000; they are the principal family of their village. But upon Mr. Bennet's death the family will face literal ruin, for they will have only a meager income of roughly £250 a year. Since his daughters have received no formal education, and have, worse, been abandoned to find their own moral levels and to gain their own insights into the way of the world within a quite limited circle, their futures after his death could by no measure be considered secure. Elizabeth's most serious error of judgment—her conviction that she is absolutely free from contingency—can be traced to her miseducation by her ironic, withdrawn father. In the event Mr. Bennet's grave mismanagement topples into disrepute only one daughter out of five, and Elizabeth's deft success salvages even that daughter from her otherwise certain oblivion.

Elizabeth is distinguished from her sisters by her special place in her father's affections; if she has "improved" herself it has been under privileged circumstances. To what extent is she responsible for the making of her own character? After Lydia's fall, and after Elizabeth realizes she loves Darcy but before his second proposal, she gives us her opinion of the value of their potential relationship:

> It was an union that must have been to the advantage of both; by her ease and liveliness, his mind might have been softened, his manners improved; and from his judgment, information, and knowledge of the world, she must have received benefit of greater importance.

But no such happy marriage could now teach the admiring multitude what connubial felicity really was. [III, chap. 8, 312]

Burke's "swinish multitude" is too famous a phrase to let us pass "admiring multitude" without a wince. Perhaps the sentence is self-mocking? In the context of Elizabeth's stream of thought, at that particular point in the novel, it appears to be so. But it is not ironic insofar as it represents the novel's final judgment. Elizabeth's marriage to Darcy, too, is the grandest marriage in all of Austen's novels. Yet, even if the marriage "teaches" us what Elizabeth says it does, can we take seriously the benefits to Elizabeth which she here anticipates? We are willing to believe it will do Darcy good. We *see* the change in him after the traumatic scene of his initial rejection; and the opening of upper-class life to welcome the inclusion of the liveliness, energy, and substance of the "middle ranks," especially of Elizabeth's moneyed relations the Gardiners, seems, in the novel as in the actual society, a saving (and necessary) enlargement. But if Darcy's reward is an Elizabeth who will literally and figuratively improve him and his estate, Elizabeth's reward seems to be more a symbolic than a real Darcy. She marries the richest man in all of Austen's novels, one feels, not so much because she needs him to save her from genteel poverty as because his wealth is the material equivalent of her moral "worth." She gets what she deserves (whereas Darcy seems to get more than he deserves).[5]

Yet it is true that, in a novel of extraordinary symmetry, we *see* Elizabeth change too. And I believe that while Darcy's change is more dramatic, hers is more profound and comes closer to a transformation of the self. Characteristic of

5. D. J. Greene's "Jane Austen and the Peerage," *PMLA*, 68 (December, 1953), 1017–1131, offers an ingenious analysis of the names in *Pride and Prejudice*, especially the exclusive "Fitzwilliam," and argues that "the unifying thesis of Jane Austen's novels is the rise of the middle-class" (p. 1028). See as well Mark Schorer, "Pride Unprejudiced," *Kenyon Review*, 18 (Winter 1956), 72–91.

Elizabeth in the first half of the novel, before Darcy's first proposal, is this remark: "'The more I see of the world, the more I am dissatisfied with it'" (II, chap. 1, 135). She delights in the ridiculous, loves to laugh at foolishness, believes in her full capacity for a full life on her own terms. She carries the aspirations for self-fulfillment of the novel, and thus also its complaint against her society and its strict fencing of the self. The novel lets us understand that these are attributes of a youthful vivacity. However that may be, the novel also demonstrates that these attributes are disrespectful of mere power, rank, and authority. Charlotte Lucas, dangerously old at twenty-seven, and plain to boot, cannot so easily ignore the real distinctions of their world:

> "[Darcy's] pride . . . does not offend *me* so much as pride often does, because there is an excuse for it. One cannot wonder that so very fine a young man, with family, fortune, everything in his favor, should think highly of himself. If I may so express it, he has a *right* to be proud."
>
> "That is very true," replied Elizabeth, "and I could easily forgive *his* pride, if he had not mortified *mine*." [I, chap. 5, 20]

We can hardly avoid being charmed by Elizabeth's response and delighted by her democratic, sharp sense of her own value. The fact is, however, that hers is a judgment based on little "information" and less "knowledge of the world." She responds as an observer, a critic of the stuck-up rich man Darcy; nothing is at issue here for her, she thinks, either personally or ideologically. The extent to which she is wrong indicates the extent to which she changes.

For Elizabeth moves from dissatisfaction with the world—her stance as an outsider—to a key role of power in the arrangements of the world, now unquestionably "her" world. It is possible for the sharp Elizabeth Bennet to mock the powerful Mr. Darcy when all this is, for her, a game. But it is not possible for the future Mrs. Darcy, looking at the world from *his* point of view within Pemberley, to do so. To reign at

Pemberley requires a retreat from irony and a habituation to gravity. A short while after learning from Darcy the truth about Wickham, Elizabeth also learns from Lydia that Mary King has been sent, for safety's sake, to Liverpool. So, Lydia exclaims, "'Wickham is safe.'"

> "And Mary King is safe!" Elizabeth added; "safe from a connection imprudent as to fortune."
>
> "But I hope there is no strong attachment on either side," said Jane.
> "I am sure there is not on *his* [said Lydia]. I will answer for it, he never cared three straws about her—who *could* about such a nasty little freckled thing?"
> Elizabeth was shocked to think that, however incapable of such coarseness of *expression* herself, the coarseness of the *sentiment* was little other than her own breast had formerly harboured and fancied liberal! [II, chap. 16, 220; Austen's italics]

Elizabeth does not say (or think), as we might expect, that Mary King is safe from marriage to a scoundrel—that is, she does not object to Wickham in the terms she spoke earlier of Darcy: merely personal terms. She does not consider the averted marriage as a marriage merely between two individuals. Rather she now employs what was previously an alien, even a mocked, vocabulary.[6] Elizabeth is shocked that previously her inner tongue had been as free and loose as Lydia's public chatter. She is aware of a new gravity in herself, a new measurement of value. She has already moved a considerable distance away from her stance as observer to an identification

---

6. As in this exchange between Mrs. Gardiner and Elizabeth:
"But my dear Elizabeth," she added, "what sort of girl is Miss King? I should be sorry to think our friend mercenary."
"Pray, my dear aunt, what is the difference in matrimonial affairs between the mercenary and the prudent motive? Where does discretion end, and avarice begin? Last Christmas you were afraid of his marrying me, because it would be imprudent; and now, because he is trying to get a girl with only ten thousand pounds, you want to find out that he is mercenary." [II, chap. 4, 152]

with power and authority: Mary King is "safe from a connection imprudent as to fortune."

Later, objecting to her father that Lydia ought not to be
allowed a trip to Brighton, she says to him: "'Our importance,
our respectability in the world must be affected by the wild
volatility, the assurance and disdain of all restraint which
mark Lydia's character'" (II, chap. 18, 231). Such a judgment,
in such terms, put in such a manner, would be entirely out of
character before the upheaval caused by Darcy's proposal and
Elizabeth's subsequent change of heart. In this interview
Elizabeth disengages herself from her father; he maintains a
distant irony toward events of which she no longer approves,
and which she sees already to be incompatible with the role
she begins seriously to consider (or now seriously believes she
has lost): her role as Darcy's wife and thus lady of the manor at
Pemberley.

In the main discussion of education in *Pride and Prejudice*—
at Netherfield when Elizabeth is visiting to tend to her ill
sister Jane—we can make a distinction between accomplishments and improvement. Accomplishments are a kind of
demonstrable knowledge, the kind that the champion of accomplishments, Miss Bingley, herself epitomizes. But besides
these accomplishments, besides "'a certain something in [a
woman's] air and manner of walking,'" Darcy argues, "'she
must yet add something more substantial, in the improvement
of her mind by extensive reading'" (I, chap. 8, 39). The
suggestion here, despite Elizabeth's objection to the number of
things Darcy and Miss Bingley include in a woman's education, is that such reading will substantially determine the nature of an individual: the improvement will be basic, rather
than, as in the case of accomplishments, a flauntable but ex-
terior clutch of attributes. The source of improvement here, as
in *Sandford and Merton*, is individual activity. But *Pride and
Prejudice* is not as egalitarian a book as *Sandford and Merton* and
neither is its author an unequivocal enthusiast of the middle
class. *Pride and Prejudice* is the great representative novel of the

major transition between the system, real and wished for, of the early eighteenth century and the new industrial and agricultural capitalism. It is written, in a sense, at a fixed point of transition, and so manages a wholesale reconciliation across a range of issues, literary and ideological.

Thus, although the novel is essentially affirmative and optimistic, its clearest educational statement is that circumstance makes character. The statement is made explicit in Elizabeth's judgment of her father and Darcy's judgment of himself—and I believe there is no question that both opinions echo the author's own view. Such a view contains the radical implication that a change of circumstance can effect a change in character, but in the novel this idea receives a conservative coloring. For circumstance in *Pride and Prejudice* tends to mean the world we are born into, a world that is at once the past and a world over which we have no effective control. In this sense the clearest source of value in the novel is, as it were, inherited value. For this reason the adult society that Mr. Bennet represents is criticized for having miseducated its children, for not having actively or adequately conditioned the environment of growth.

The source of value in this view, as well as of failure, is clear enough. But it is also wholly paternal. The father, insofar as he represents social authority, is in control, and is criticized for errors in his exercise of control (or lack of it). But cannot the children, as individuals, make their own lives? Paradoxically, the paternalistic model is affirmed as the source of value at the same time that the two actual fathers are shown to have failed, in varying degrees, to fulfill their roles. In order to reproduce the vitality of the social system, then, in some sense the children *must* make their own way. We see them doing so; and, at least for Elizabeth and Darcy, the assurance of value is gained only after traumatic experience. Once trauma has been survived and error worked through to a new grasp on self and society, then the basis of a reconciliation that strengthens inherited value has been laid.

In our experience of reading the novel we are, I think, wholly convinced that this reconciliation is plausible and right. Yet it is clear, once we lift our eyes from the page, that this is a reconciliation made within very careful limits.[7] Darcy and Elizabeth, for instance, no doubt learn from bitter experience; but even this learning has a passive quality: Elizabeth "teaches" Darcy a "lesson"; Elizabeth "receives benefit" from Darcy's "judgment, information, and knowledge of the world." The final triumph in the novel, too, is visualized as Pemberley. Now Pemberley may be Darcy's home, Darcy's estate, and may thus mean "Darcy" to Elizabeth. But Pemberley in fact is as much, if not more, the "soil" of the late Mr. Darcy; an estate is not built up in a year or two. So that while the novel demonstrates the failures of Mr. Darcy and Mr. Bennet, and forces their children to make their own way, in the end all of the reconciliations are focused on Pemberley, which, as it were, takes them in and makes itself stronger. All of the different personalities and the different ways of life they represent—the Bingleys, the Gardiners, the Bennets, even Lady Catherine—all are concentrated into Pemberley. So that the reconciliations obscure and overcome the failures of the novel's paternalistic society and thereby apotheosize it. Elizabeth and Darcy may, through their activity, have substantially changed themselves, or, in the language of the novel, improved themselves; but it is the unchanged past embodied in Pemberley that actually triumphs.

When Jane Austen writes under greater strain, in a more defensive posture, as in *Mansfield Park*, the primacy of the landed estate becomes unpleasant dogma. The interplay be-

7. A. Walton Litz finds Darcy and Elizabeth's marriage satisfying not because of the union of the two individuals but because "their marriage is a complete fulfillment of the novel's artistic imperatives"; but he believes this "was a triumph not to be repeated, one that was replaced in the later novels by less comforting views of human nature." See his "Into the Nineteenth Century: *Pride and Prejudice*," in *Twentieth-Century Interpretations of "Pride and Prejudice*," ed. E. Rubinstein (Englewood Cliffs, N.J.: Prentice-Hall, 1969), p. 63.

tween the activity of the children and the responsibility of the
adults stops; the novel is more insistent but less certain about
the source of value.

Shortly after she arrives in the country Mary Crawford
sends for her harp but cannot get it easily conveyed to her
sister's house because of the late hay harvest. Neither farmer
nor laborer will fetch it for her, and they are offended that she
asks.

"'I shall understand all your ways in time; but coming down
with the true London maxim, that every thing is to be got with
money, I was a little embarrassed at first by the sturdy independence of your country customs'" (I, chap. 6, 58). This is
an ingenious damning passage. We can believe that Mary—
who, if she really was embarrassed at first, was surely ur-
banely supercilious at last—would without any sense of self-
exposure have proclaimed the London maxim to be what no
doubt it was, that everything is to be got with money. But
Jane Austen's identification of this maxim with London dis-
torts the truth: it is, for example, Tom Bertram's maxim too.
A good deal of the money in London was the money of the
landed rich. And "sturdy independence" are not Mary's but
Austen's words. They inject into Mary's own damning account of herself the system of value that damns her. It is hard
to believe that she would have named the system in this way,
for she is not, certainly at this early point in the novel, apt to
take the country and its ways seriously, or differently than she
takes everything else—with a touch of irony. "Country customs" might be the words of both Jane Austen and her citified
creation Mary. They, too, however, tend toward the hyperbole of "sturdy independence"; they are a part of the in-
dulgence allowed eulogies of the countryside. But the distinction between money and custom is not conveyed strongly
enough if we assume our own, contemporary, weakened
meaning of custom. For the distinction is no less than a distinction in systems and perceptions of value. For Mary money
is a kind of magic, and gets you anything you want. That

money converts into labor may, in some vague way, be apparent to her, but in the event she is blind to the reverse of the equation: that labor becomes money. For the farmers and laborers, moreover, labor is valuable directly for what it does: collect the harvest. That this labor will later translate into money seems less important than that collecting the harvest must happen at a particular time if the rural system is to be maintained. At harvesttime, consequently, money is not desirable, for it in effect cancels out labor, which is. Mary Crawford asks the country laborers to remove themselves from productive labor to a kind of service role—to withdraw, in other words, into a wholly money economy. This expectation is what is resisted and resented. For this reason Mary Crawford's autonomy from the country system of value creates a clash of meanings in the novel which finally leaves her isolated from Mansfield in the corrupted world of London moneyed society.

But whereas the clash of values is clear and brilliantly exploited in this early scene, the novel rarely reaches this level of clarity. The clarity here derives from the solid continuity between actual relationships and activities on the one hand and consciousness on the other. It is no mystery why bailiff, farmers, and laborers are offended at Mary or why Mary should so gracelessly have ventured offense. It is clear why the country people, who are here shown immersed in the labor of the countryside, should have a certain world view; and it is equally clear why Mary has a different one. But consider this remark by Fanny, upon hearing she may have to quit Mansfield and take up residence with the voracious Mrs. Norris. She has been confiding in her good, bland cousin Edmund: "'I am very much obliged to you for trying to reconcile me to what must be. If I could suppose my aunt really to care for me, it would be delightful to feel myself of consequence to any body!—*Here*, I know I am of none, and yet I love the place so well'" (I, chap. 3, 27; Austen's italics). One is more than willing to agree that life under the same roof as Mrs. Norris would be unbearable (as Jane Austen demonstrates when she locks the sinning Maria in with her), and that for Fanny the loss of Edmund in exchange for Mrs. Norris can hardly have seemed promising. But this is not the point Austen wishes to make. The point she makes is that Fanny loves Mansfield Park. Why? Sir Thomas is formal, cool, officious, and distant; his wife immobilized on her couch; Mrs. Norris, her surrogate, is insolent and nasty; Tom Bertram pays little attention to her, gambles, is a scapegrace; the two sisters Maria and Julia think too well of themselves to think much of her except when they need a third for games or walks. That leaves Edmund, and even he is away much of the year, and can in any event hardly be equated with Mansfield Park. What, then, is the source of Fanny's love of Mansfield? How are we to make sense of the non sequitur *"Here,* I know I am of none [of no consequence], and yet I love the place so well"? Can we really believe she means what Edmund takes her to mean, that she will miss the park and gardens? But then, as he says, that is just what she would *not* quit.

The obscure virtue of Mansfield Park as an institution (see my discussion below and in Chapter 4) is at one with the obscure "justification" of the character Fanny Price. The overt educational argument of *Mansfield Park* repeats—more forcefully, for this is a dogmatic novel, in which ideology *must* dominate character and action—the overt argument of *Pride and Prejudice:* circumstance determines character. Sir Thomas, at once more powerful, more active, more responsible, more symbolic—in short, more paternal—than Mr. Bennet, commits errors of greater magnitude and suffers a more thorough rebuke at the hands of fate and the author. The guardian of an endangered way of life and of a system of value threatened from within and without, he fails in his main responsibility: to ensure, within his family, the reproduction of value.[8] When

8. For a discussion of Sir Thomas's responsibility, see Marvin Mudrick's chapter on *Mansfield Park* in his *Jane Austen: Irony as Defense and Discovery* (Berkeley: University of California Press, 1968 [first published 1952 by Princeton University Press]).

his poor niece Fanny Price is about to take up residence in his mansion, among his daughters and his sons, he is anxious lest her "'disposition be really bad.'" If this proves to be the case, she must not, for the children's (especially the girls') sake, be allowed to "'continue... in the family.'" But he doubts this *will* be the case; Mrs. Norris amiably assures him that "'it will be an education for the child... only being with her cousins'" (I, chap. 1, 10). But we learn soon enough that these same genteel exemplars Maria and Julia are "deficient in the less common acquirements of self-knowledge, generosity, and humility. In every thing but disposition, they were admirably taught" (I, chap. 2, 55). At the end of the novel, rendering judgment on himself, Sir Thomas says that "he had meant them to be good, but his cares had been directed to the understanding and manners, not the disposition; and of the necessity of self-denial and humility, he feared they had never heard from any lips that could profit them" (III, chap. 17, 463). Having failed in his duty, Sir Thomas yet remains the patriarchal figure; abandoned by his eldest son and his two daughters, finding even the sound and sensible Edmund imperfect, he embraces at last the person he feared, misjudged, and ignored at first and, almost, throughout: Fanny. How does the novel account for the making of her disposition?

Three circumstances in Fanny's life are intended as formative: her life as a child at Portsmouth, her place as a dependent at Mansfield Park, and her tutorial education by Edmund. When Fanny first arrives at Portsmouth she is homesick for her family and the people she loves. That is, she feels as Austen believes she ought; but when, later, we follow her to Portsmouth, her devotion as a ten-year-old girl and her repulsion as an eighteen-year-old woman are hard to square. I will discuss these opposing reactions below. In the first volume of the novel, however, Fanny's origins show themselves to be formative insofar as they make her reticent, unsure, shy, abashed in her new quarters. For the modern reader the difference between Portsmouth and Mansfield may not seem as striking as it must have seemed to Fanny; but a glance at the painting of Harleston Park, ostensibly the original of Mansfield Park, which R. W. Chapman provides in his Oxford edition will make the difference more graphic. What is involved is an extraordinary change, and it is not surprising that Fanny, even at eighteen, is not wholly comfortable in her adopted home and treasures her small rooms in the neglected upper regions of the mansion. Moreover, Fanny's situation must in other ways be extremely uncomfortable: she is one of the family, but she is also a penniless dependent; she shares in the life of the house, but always takes the last place; she has available the expanse of Mansfield, the gardens, the park, the neighborhood, the entire impressive wealth of perquisites that life as a member of a rich and powerful country family brings with it—but she enjoys them, as it were, on charity. She can never be certain what is and what is not *rightfully* hers. She can never be certain when Mrs. Norris or Lady Bertram will ask her to perform a servant's work.

Sir Thomas is concerned, initially, that his daughters welcome Fanny generously while yet maintaining an inequality between them—this is a point of "'great delicacy,'" as he tells Mrs. Norris (I, chap. 1, 10). Mrs. Norris's delicacy, however, cannot have been the admiration of the neighborhood: we are not surprised that "Fanny was often mortified by their [Maria's and Julia's] treatment of her" (I, chap. 2, 20). The nature of the situation and the inevitable superciliousness of the welcoming family overcome—initially—all good intentions. Initially—and at the hands of Mrs. Norris until the very end—Fanny is treated at Mansfield the same way, at heart, as Jane Eyre is treated at Gateshead. The surprise is that, cruel as her treatment might be, "she thought too lowly of her own claims to feel injured by it" (I, chap. 2, 20). The surprise is that, although she is of no consequence to anyone, she loves the place so well. The surprise is that, from start to finish, Fanny displays a developed disposition and embodies the system of value of Mansfield Park itself.

The novel attributes to Edmund the training of Fanny's mind.

Kept back as she was by every body else, his single support
could not bring her forward, but his attentions were otherwise
of the highest importance in assisting the improvement of her
mind, and extending its pleasures. He knew her to be clever, to
have a quick apprehension as well as good sense, and a fond-
ness for reading, which, properly directed, must be an education in itself. Miss Lee taught her French, and heard her read
her daily portion of History; but he recommended the books
which charmed her leisure hours, he encouraged her taste, and
corrected her judgment; he made reading useful by talking to
her of what she read, and heightened its attraction by judicious
praise. In return for such services she loved him better than
any body in the world except William; her heart was divided
between the two.   [I, chap. 2, 22]

This passage must bear much weight; in effect, it must explain, it must "justify" Fanny's character. The impact on
Fanny of her home in Portsmouth and her alienation at Mansfield Park are themes subdued and insinuated into the novel;
Edmund's active tutorship, on the contrary, is offered in a
specially emphatic way: he was "of the highest importance in
assisting the improvement of her mind." Jane Austen does not
mean only intellect; she means, in the words of the novel,
disposition, the whole bent, the essential nature of a person.
But whereas we might accept the proposition that Edmund, as
Fanny's tutor, had trained her intellect, we are imposed on if
we must believe that, by the mere instrument of a discussion
of books, he formed her nature. We are imposed on especially
because, even if we were to grant this notion to be plausible,
we never see any moral training, of the kind suggested in the
passage above, in the action of the novel. Fanny quotes
Cowper, but she never discusses him with Edmund. And it is
clear that the novel itself views the essentials of disposition as
necessitating an engagement far broader than any course of
reading. When, in an important passage at the end of the novel
to which I have already made reference, Sir Thomas asks
himself what has been "the most direful mistake in his plan of
education," he concludes

principle, active principle, had been wanting... they [Maria
and Julia] had never been taught to govern their inclinations
and tempers, by that sense of duty which can alone suffice.
They had been instructed theoretically in their religion, but
never required to bring it into daily practice.... He had meant
them to be good, but his cares had been directed to the understanding and manners, not the disposition; and of the necessity
of self-denial and humility, he feared they had never heard
from any lips that could profit them.   [III, chap. 17, 463]

In *Pride and Prejudice* Darcy proposes improvement in the
manner in which Edmund administers it: by reading—
although Edmund's involvement with Fanny's reading seems
thorough rather than a superficial consignment of a list of
classics. But in *Pride and Prejudice* the actual improvement of
the main characters does not occur through reading but
through experience, or rather through the interaction of experience and personality. In *Mansfield Park*, too, the conclu-
sive teacher is said to be practice: not theoretical instruction
but daily performance; not understanding or manner but disposition. The valued attributes are not in themselves, it is
true, attractive: duty, self-denial, humility; but I wish to leave
the moral intention of the novel to one side for the moment,
and look instead at the way the novel argues value is created.
Sir Thomas's self-criticism states the novel's definitive view;
but if Sir Thomas accurately analyzes what was lacking in the
education of his daughters, he does not, by implication, show
us what positively contributed to the contrary results in the
growth of Fanny. Moreover, Sir Thomas's reflections take the
shape of, and speak in the voice of, mere moral prescription.
More seriously wanting than Sir Thomas's summary allows is
any view of the self's active creation of the self. The conservative coloring of the idea that circumstance makes character
comes close, in *Mansfield Park*, to a view in which the individual is a totally passive recipient of character. Consequently
Sir Thomas's reflection may provide him with a lesson for
other patriarchs but it says little about the actual education of

daughters or about the ability of children to make their own lives.

> That Julia escaped better than Maria was owing, in some measure, to a favorable difference of disposition and circumstance, but in a greater to her having been less the darling of that very aunt, less flattered, and less spoilt. Her beauty and acquirements had held but a second place. She had been always used to think herself a little inferior to Maria. Her temper was naturally the easiest of the two, her feelings, though quick, were more controllable; and education had not given her so very hurtful a degree of self-consequence. [III, chap. 17, 466]

In short, Julia had nothing to do with it.

But how, then, to account for Fanny? She is Austen's avatar of Constance of Chaucer's "Man of Law's Tale": while all around her fail or totter, she holds steady, never wavering from her virtuous course.[9] Of all the characters in the novel, even Edmund and Sir Thomas, only Fanny properly values Mansfield and accurately judges what it is due. Her definitive assessment comes at Portsmouth:

> The elegance, propriety, regularity, harmony—and perhaps, above all, the peace and tranquillity of Mansfield, were brought to her remembrance every hour of the day, by the prevalence of every thing opposite to them *here*.
> ... At Mansfield, no sounds of contention, no raised voice, no abrupt bursts, no tread of violence was ever heard; all proceeded in a regular course of cheerful orderliness; every body had their due importance; every body's feelings were consulted. If tenderness could ever be supposed wanting, good sense and good breeding supplied its place; and as to the little irritations, sometimes introduced by aunt Norris, they were short, they were trifling, they were as a drop of water to the ocean, compared with the ceaseless tumult of her present abode. [III, chap. 8, 391]

There is no hint of irony or discordance in this passage: Fanny and Jane Austen mean what it says; we are not intended to

---

9. In a serious vein this is Lionel Trilling's view in his sophistical "*Mansfield Park*"; see *The Opposing Self* (New York: Viking Press, 1955).

raise our eyebrows and smile at Fanny's special pleading for Mansfield. But although the contrast between tumult and tranquillity concurs with our reading experience, the qualities associated with Mansfield's tranquillity come wholly out of the air. "Cheerful orderliness"? Of whom is Fanny speaking? Of the stern Sir Thomas? Of the restrained Edmund? Of the recumbent Lady Bertram? Of Mrs. Norris, Maria, Julia, Tom? Of herself? Order there may be, but cheerfulness there is not. "Every body had their due importance; every body's feelings were consulted." For the inner circle of the family this is superficially true; but only in small things. In the major crisis of her life, her decision to marry Rushworth, were Maria's feelings truly consulted? Did Tom give Edmund his due importance? The glaring exception to this alluring retrospect, however, is Fanny herself. She pleads for Mansfield in open contradiction of her own experience. "If tenderness could ever be supposed wanting, good sense and good breeding supplied its place." Tenderness, however, was usually wanting, and the good sense of the book is concentrated—at least in the book's own terms—in Fanny herself. After this, the deft devaluation of Mrs. Norris to the rank of a mere irritant—contradicted by the novel's final meting out of reward and punishment—is hardly surprising.

In the most substantial recent account of *Mansfield Park*, Alastair M. Duckworth assesses the passages above as follows: "In Fanny's 'review of the two houses' . . . we discover not the rejection of her home by one who has acquired gentility, but the recognition of a contrast between a cultural space which—in spite of the deficiencies of its inhabitants—retains order, stability, and harmony, and a cultural space which, through gross parental indolence and indifference, has become a Hobbesian state of incivility."[10] Duckworth's reading of *Mansfield Park* is the most thorough and, because of its perceptive social orientation, the most illuminating that I know of. Neverthe-

10. Alastair M. Duckworth, *The Improvement of the Estate: A Study of Jane Austen's Novels* (Baltimore: Johns Hopkins Press, 1971), p. 77.

less, his judgment here is seriously wrong. In effect
Duckworth repeats, in an elegant language of interpretation,
the mystifications of Austen. A "cultural space" is not a
mountain or a river gorge: its substance derives from the
people who occupy it and create relationships within it. The
pattern of life defines the "cultural space." Now the difference
between Portsmouth and Mansfield Park is a difference of
class; crudely in the novel, of wealth.[11] The novel, moreover,
was written at a time when the notion of class was being
developed and when the distinctions among ways of life
rooted in class experience had already entered the ensuing
prolonged period of sharp conflict. Consequently the depic-
tion of Portsmouth is very heavily loaded. Here Fanny has
just received a letter from Mary Crawford: "In her present
exile from good society, and distance from every thing that
had been wont to interest her, a letter from one belonging to
the set where her heart lived, written with affection, and some
degree of elegance, was thoroughly acceptable" (III, chap. 9,
393). Can this passage be given any other reading but as the
sentiment of someone grown genteel who now rejects her
home? But this rejection itself is not out of the ordinary, nor
would we normally be shocked by it—it reflects, after all, the
experience of becoming *déclassé*, which has since Austen's time

11. Mary Lascelles, in *Jane Austen and Her Art* (London: Oxford University Press, 1939), writes interestingly that whereas Austen means us to feel
for her other heroines "as we feel for friends and lovers," for Fanny she
means us to feel "as for a creature less well furnished for offence and defence
than those with which it is compelled to live. Among the Bertrams she is like
a mortal among giants. That is why . . . we are allowed first to make her
acquaintance when she is a child. . . . It is tenderness as towards a child that
is implied in Jane Austen's use of a phrase exceptional with her—'my
Fanny'" (p. 215). Perhaps. But what distinguishes Fanny from Austen's
other heroines is class: *that* is how she differs from Elizabeth or Emma. She
is the only heroine whom Austen does not *know* but must imagine. And she
imagines, I believe, looking down. Only in Fanny do we see a heroine
behaving as she *ought* rather than as Austen knows she would. There is
perhaps pity and protectiveness but there is also some condescension in
Austen's "my Fanny."

spread widely through our societies; rather, one objects to the hostility expressed toward Portsmouth and the animosity against it which the novel, and the novelist, indulge the better to raise Mansfield. For, if we eliminate the distance and prejudice of a class perspective, the Prices are no more "indolent and indifferent" than the Bertrams. After their own fashion, the Prices express affection and concern—certainly for William. They treat Fanny pretty much as Fanny was initially treated at Mansfield Park.

If the difference between Mansfield Park and Portsmouth is a difference of class,[12] to call one a state of order and harmony and the other of Hobbesian incivility is to mystify the real distinction. Life at Portsmouth, after all, is given shape and character by Jane Austen in a novel that wishes to celebrate the life of the landed gentry. *Mansfield Park* meets the dangers of the transformation of society by beating back the Crawfords into immorality and rootless urbanity on the one hand, and by beating back the Prices into a bestial, grimy state of nature on the other. What remains, or emerges in conclusion, is Mansfield Park and Fanny Price/Bertram. But just as the actual source of Mansfield Park's value is in this way obscured and hidden, so is the making of Fanny. Fanny springs upon the novel full grown. Unlike Elizabeth Bennet, she never engages the world to make herself: she is made already, and as the alternative heroes and heroines fail and fall away, she emerges and triumphs—by default, as it were. Even the novel's con-

12. Mudrick calls it "proletarian Portsmouth" (*Jane Austen*, p. 155). This phrase is very far off the mark; the Prices, with their two servants and their very rich relations, are hardly working class; and their relation to industrial capitalism is not obvious. But if this is a sloppy use of language, it yet states the difference of class, and points to the basic dissimilarity of the communities. Which distinguishes it very favorably indeed from Tony Tanner's account of the different locales of action in the novel, locales he takes to be simply "symbolic." In Tanner's account symbols float about in the air, well above the action, and their roots in the actual activity of the novel have somehow nothing to do with meaning. See Tanner's introduction to the Penguin *Mansfield Park* (Harmondsworth, 1966).

servative account of education fails to explain Fanny. The only substantial evidence of her education is her reading under Edward's tutorship, a tutorship that, in the extended crisis of the novel, she transcends without any transcending effort, without any "building" of character that we are allowed to see. Elizabeth Bennet is a creature of an optimistic, energetic mode: she will bring light, life, and energy to the depleted, rigid world of the Darcys and the de Bourghs. But Fanny is created in defense of an establishment: *Mansfield Park* is narrated not from the point of view of Longbourn, from the view outside the estate walls, but from within. In *Pride and Prejudice* Longbourn and Pemberley are reconciled. In *Mansfield Park* Portsmouth is annihilated. And although Fanny is even more an outsider than Elizabeth, she props up Mansfield by her solidity, her tranquillity, her immovable certainty in the catchwords of Mansfield Park: self-denial, humility, duty, order, peace. That these qualities also promote harmony is the novel's argument, the final quality without which the others cannot rise to meaning. But the novel does not demonstrate that they do rise to harmony; this notion is asserted, asserted finally, in Fanny's reflection at Portsmouth, by a thorough distortion of the novel's action. Value in *Mansfield Park*, then, derives more or less by magic; it is not made, it is not the product of human relationships. Mansfield is a cultural space—but a space only, a house and grounds, an expanse of elegant chambers. Similarly Fanny is a character without justification: she merely is. How she has come to be what she is remains a mystery.

III

This is something we could under no circumstances say of Jane Eyre, although the two characters have, as far as their circumstances go, much in common. Indeed, Avrom Fleishman, in his study of *Mansfield Park*, suggests that, despite important differences of sensibility, "*Jane Eyre* stands among the progeny of *Mansfield Park* by its sustained focus on the young girl from the provinces finding her way through the world, experiencing the inner drama of moral and sexual impulses, and overcoming her limitations—both internal and external—through a sustained exercise of moral will that makes her a heroine."[13] The suggestion is of a continuity of genre. If we accept this suggestion—and I think we can—we are impressed by the tremendous chasm between the books as well. In *Mansfield Park* Jane Austen makes reference to *Rasselas* and finds there a witty Dr. Johnson, the writer of *bons mots* (III, chap. 8, 392); but the *Rasselas* Helen Burns reads is a darkly Christian book associated with her death-tending aphorism: "'I live in calm, looking to the end'" (I, chap. 6, 59). *Mansfield Park* depicts a society in trouble and danger but free of death, anguish, and even poverty; *Jane Eyre* begins with rebellion, death, and poverty: these are its starting points. If we set Scott to one side as an exceptional figure, a writer of a genre distinct from the one in which Austen and Brontë wrote, then *Jane Eyre* takes its place as the novel in which the transformation of Jane Austen's society is registered: it is in *Jane Eyre* that industrial and agricultural capitalism first make a determining impact on the main tradition of the English novel.[14]

Jane Eyre expresses the forces of its time in a triumphant merger of Romanticism and the individualist ethic of laissez faire. Adam Smith's notion of value as the creation of labor receives here its great fictional expression: for Jane is activity itself, a character developed in startling immediacy as the product of an intense interaction between the individual and her

13. Avrom Fleishman, *A Reading of "Mansfield Park"* (Baltimore: Johns Hopkins Press, 1970), p. 72.

14. It may be argued that it is in fact in the novels of Dickens that this transformation is registered. But I don't think one can say this of the early Dickens, and the Dickens of the years 1847–48 and then the Dickens of *Hard Times* should be seen properly to come after the stage of consciousness expressed in *Jane Eyre*.

world. If the brashness of the entrepreneur may seem to contradict the political tendencies of the Romantics, yet they share a common impulse, as Steven Marcus observes in his *Engels, Manchester, and the Working Class.*

> We know now that what, among other things, [the Romantics] were experiencing... was the general form that society in their time was rapidly taking on.
>
> Self-realization... had [by the 1840s] taken on the normative shape of the pursuit of self-interest. And the universal search for self—literally self-seeking—stood revealed in its current historical embodiment as a competitive activity in which one's personal quest was achieved by means of the defeat... of the same quest in others.[15]

In *Mansfield Park* Fanny, the poor relative, the lower-class outsider, is drawn into the established family; in her search for self, she becomes not selfish but selfless, immerses herself in the flow of Bertram life and loses herself in the Bertrams' mansion until she is indistinguishable from them, indeed becomes the best of them. She represents Jane Austen's effort to push back the forces of social change into the old norms. But Jane Eyre, more abandoned than Fanny, without a family to turn to, must in fact make her own way, must make her own value. Not only do we find, in *Jane Eyre, various* established worlds, but Jane settles into none of them. The adjustment of the end of the novel is consequently far more complex than that of *Mansfield Park.* Partly Jane Eyre embodies the exhilarating spirit of individualism; she is a kind of nineteenth-century equivalent of the robust Moll Flanders. At the same time Jane's hard-gained independence does not easily yield her a social place. For she is the carrier of a revolutionary individualism, an individualism that, though it transforms the self, yet can no longer find in the world of industrial capitalism a viable social connection. If laissez faire leads in

15. Steven Marcus, *Engels, Manchester, and the Working Class* (New York: Random House, 1974), p. 156.

one direction to self-seeking and a brutal competitiveness, it leads for Jane to the ambiguous exile of Ferndean.

In an early essay, "The Old Culture and the New Culture," Georg Lukács argues that the ideology that brought the bourgeoisie to power—that of individual freedom—had to be repressed once dominance had actually been achieved. The idea of individual freedom could not be applied across the board "without the self-negation of the social order that brought this ideology into being in the first place. Briefly: it was impossible for the bourgeois class to apply its own idea of freedom to the proletariat."[16] In *Shirley*, where Charlotte Brontë attempts to meet political issues head-on, she dramatizes the split between freedom for one class and repression for another which Lukács identifies above. But in *Jane Eyre* she takes the dangerous position of celebrating individual freedom from the point of view of the working class. This was one reason for the novel's mixed reception and for the opinions of some reviewers, notably Elizabeth Rigby, that the novel cried out against the existing order in the terms of Chartism.[17]

The whole introductory sequence at Gateshead Hall is permeated by a political metaphor.

> "You ought to be aware, Miss [Bessie tells the rebellious Jane], that you are under obligations to Mrs. Reed: she keeps you: if she were to turn you off, you would have to go to the poor-house."
> I had nothing to say to these words: they were not new to me: my very first recollections of existence included hints of the same kind.   [I, chap. 2, 12–13]

Jane's "very first recollections of existence" are that she is liable at any time to fall upon the poorhouse; she is " 'less than

16. Georg Lukács, *Marxism and Human Liberation*, ed. E. San Juan, Jr. (New York: Dell, 1973), p. 9.
17. See, for instance, *Christian Remembrancer*, April 1848, and, for Elizabeth Rigby's review, *Quarterly Review*, December 1848; excerpts from both are found in *The Brontës: The Critical Heritage*, ed. Miriam Allott (London: Routledge & Kegan Paul, 1974).

a servant,'" the lady's maid Abbot tells her. It is from this standpoint that Jane rouses herself against the porcine John Reed, calling him "'slave driver'" and "'tyrant'" (I, chap. 1, 11). In this "mood of the revolted slave" (I, chap. 2, 14) Jane gives us one of the earliest glimpses in fiction of the hidden injuries of class: "Why was I always suffering, always brow-beaten, always accused, for ever condemned? Why could I never please? Why was it useless to try to win anyone's fa-vor? . . . I dared commit no fault: I strove to fulfill every duty; and I was termed naughty and tiresome, sullen and sneaking, from morning to noon, and from noon to night" (I, chap. 2, 15). She cries out against this treatment, "'Unjust!—unjust!'"; it is "insupportable oppression"; against it her "brain was in tumult and all [her] heart in insurrection!" (I, chap. 2, 15). Her suppressed outrage explodes in her climactic assault on Mrs. Reed, one of the great anti-authoritarian moments in the Victorian novel: ". . . my soul began to expand, to exult, with the strangest sense of freedom, of triumph, I ever felt. It seemed as if an invisible bond had burst, and that I had strug-gled out into unhoped-for liberty" (I, chap. 4, 37). The claims of individual freedom, here at the earliest of the novel's moments of sudden opening out, of expansion into new pos-sibilities, are not abstractly put; rather the revolted slave, the girl who is less than a servant, rises up, bursts her bonds, and triumphs over authority. The making of fictional character occurs, then, in *Jane Eyre* in an especially intense and loaded form; in a manner altogether more concrete and thorough than either Elizabeth or Fanny, Jane will make her life by a pro-found transformation of self and the self's society.

But if the main thrust of the novel is toward a rebellious self-fulfillment, a persistent countertheme is voiced by Helen Burns and, in a more tempered way, by Miss Temple.[18]

18. Terry Eagleton, in his ground-breaking *Myths of Power: A Marxist Study of the Brontës* (London: Macmillan, 1975), writes (p. 4):
We find embedded in Charlotte's work . . . a constant struggle be-tween two ambiguous, internally divided sets of values. On the one

Elizabeth Rigby complained that she found in the novel "a murmuring against the comforts of the rich and against the privations of the poor, which... is a murmuring against God's appointment."[19] Jane's rebellion amounts to a claim of equality and the self's due within the arrangements of the living world; but Helen, in a powerful traditional Christian mode, maintains exactly an opposite view, much in the terms of Elizabeth Rigby. The novel pays heed to the *Christianity* of this view; yet self-denial, self-repression, submission—Fanny's qualities—mean in *Jane Eyre* one's utter surrender to an obnoxious social order—to Mrs. Reed, Brocklehurst, Blanche Ingram, St. John Rivers.

The novel uneasily acknowledges this meaning, but even while it excoriates conventional distinctions of class and the hypocritical ideology of self-denial that those in authority preach to others, it nonetheless reveres those who submit rather

---

hand are ranged the values of rationality, coolness, shrewd self-seeking, energetic individualism, radical protest and rebellion; on the other hand lie the habits of piety, submission, culture, tradition, conservatism.... It is possible to decipher in the conflicts between [these values] a fictionally transformed version of the tensions and alliances between the two social classes which dominated the Brontës' world: the industrial bourgeoisie and the landed gentry or aristocracy. I read Charlotte's novels as "myths" which work towards a balance or fusion of blunt bourgeois rationality and flamboyant Romanticism, brash initiative and genteel cultivation, passionate rebellion and cautious conformity; and those interchanges embody a complex structure of convergence and antagonism between the landed and industrial sectors of the contemporary ruling class.

This insight is very helpful, though more helpful for the novels other than *Jane Eyre*. If we take Eagleton's list of opposites, we find, paradoxically, "flamboyant Romanticism" included with "genteel cultivation" and "cautious conformity" to comprise the landed values. This juxtaposition is puzzling. The jointure of Romanticism and laissez faire in *Jane Eyre* is better explained, I believe, by Marcus's analysis of self-seeking. Moreover, Eagleton evades the exuberant, wonderfully satisfying individualism of *Jane Eyre* and its profoundly radical thrust. He does so partly, I believe, because he fails to give the novel's feminism adequate notice. For all that, this is the best analysis of the Brontës that we have.

19. Allott, *The Brontës*, p. 109.

than rebel. Especially puzzling and important in this regard is Miss Temple. In *Jane Eyre* the educational message of Austen's books, that circumstance makes character, receives a radical interpretation; for, on the whole, Jane creates her own circumstances or, if circumstances oppress her, revolts against them or struggles to transform them. But although in *Jane Eyre* the social world is subject to change alongside the individual, the one fixed world to which Jane Eyre submits is Lowood School under the guidance of Maria Temple. Insofar as Jane "receives" an education, she receives it there.

But one can say with far less clarity than in Fanny's case what that education amounts to. Before the typhoid epidemic we have two impressions of Lowood: the first is of it as an "institution," that is, as a boarding school with a certain regimentation and routine. The excesses of this routine, with its hypocritical intention, in Brocklehurst's words, of making the girls " 'hardy, patient, self-denying' " (I, chap. 7, 63), matter less than that it is routine. For Fanny's education, like Elizabeth Bennet's, occurs still in the home and follows the pattern of upper-class life; the education of Austen's men at Eton and Oxford is mentioned but never dramatized. So that whatever accomplishments may be boasted, they appear, in the novels, to have been simply "picked up." But Jane goes to school. Even before Helen Burns's death Jane's initial account of a harsh, grinding regimen punctuated by bells, burned meals, and punishment gives way to a pleased emphasis on learning. Once Mr. Lloyd clears her name with Miss Temple, Jane resolves "to pioneer [her] way" through every difficulty: "I toiled hard, and my success was proportionate to my efforts; my memory . . . improved with practice . . . in a few weeks I was promoted to a higher class; in less than two months I was allowed to commence French and drawing." On the basis of this entirely intellectual account Jane declares, "I would not now have changed Lowood with all its privations, for Gateshead and its daily luxuries" (I, chap. 8, 75).

If, for Jane, French and drawing, the latter especially, are far from what they might have been to Miss Bingley—mere accomplishments—yet they do not go far toward explaining her moral training. We get this only in an abbreviated account once Miss Temple leaves Lowood to marry the Reverend Mr. Nasmyth: "I had imbibed from her something of her nature and much of her habits; more harmonious thoughts: what seemed better regulated feelings had become the inmates of my mind. I had given in allegiance to duty and order; I was quiet; I believed I was content: to the eyes of others, usually even to my own, I appeared a disciplined and subdued character" (I, chap. 10, 85). We can read this passage to say that the revolted slave in Jane had been "disciplined." But that would be a half-truth, for it would suggest that Jane's "nature," her irreducible self, was somehow fixed and forever given. Jane's sense of self, her soaring "I," is as strong as that of any fictional character in the century; and it is an especially potent and representative "I" at the time of its creation, in the late 1840s. But this "I" grows to its mature fulfillment by means of a profound transformation, a real dialectical process of growth. So that at each stage of the novel Jane enters in a thorough way the new mode, the new level of experience offered; she enters it and it enters her; and from this exchange Jane emerges not what she was but stronger, changed, and, paradoxically, more fully herself. Jane will not, like Fanny, become absorbed by a value system not her own.

So Jane cannot become Miss Temple; she "imbibes" what Miss Temple can offer, but once Miss Temple is gone, Jane realizes immediately that it is not enough, that it will not satisfy, and longs again for "liberty" (I, chap. 10, 86). It is an index of her growth that she now understands that she can translate her longing for liberty into an actual life only by giving it concrete shape: thus she falls upon "servitude," not because she needs to be mastered or yearns for a will superior to her own—although there is some of that in Jane—but because servitude, as she says, "must be a matter of fact. Any one may serve" (I, chap. 10, 86). That is to say that Jane's

craving for liberty is neither passive nor fantastic but powerfully actual: she *must* have liberty, and thus takes the steps
available, such as they are, to get it. And so we follow Jane
through the critical process of getting herself a job.

It may be obvious that a job is not self-fulfillment, but a
glance back to Fanny or Elizabeth exposes the explosive force
of Jane's work in the novel's account of daily life. Jane's daily
life is no mystery; her engagement in the mundane necessities
that shape and form our lives culminates in a romantic alliance
quite different from those of Fanny and Elizabeth. Nonetheless, no one knows better than Jane that a job as a governess in
an isolated and vacant country house cannot be dressed up as
fulfillment. Yet she is sensitive, too, as Fanny might have
been, to what she *ought* to feel in her situation, as a woman.
For having gone the range of experience from Gateshead to
Thornfield, she knows that the Helen Burnses and the Maria
Temples, not to say the Elizabeth Rigbys, of the world will
expect her to assume her place and be still. It is against this
constricting, essentially reactionary system of feeling that Jane
formulates her great speeches for liberty; and it is from this
perspective that, as Inga-Stina Ewbank says, "Jane embodies
in herself the woman problem, the governess problem, and the
class question."[20]

> It is vain to say human beings ought to be satisfied with tran-
> quillity: they must have action; and they will make it if they
> cannot find it. Millions are condemned to a stiller doom than
> mine, and millions are in silent revolt against their lot. Nobody
> knows how many rebellions besides political rebellions fer-
> ment in the masses of life which people the earth. Women are
> supposed to be very calm generally: but women feel just as
> men feel; they need exercise for their faculties, and a field for
> their efforts as much as their brothers do; they suffer from too
> rigid a constraint, too absolute a stagnation, precisely as men
> would suffer; and it is narrow-minded in their more privileged

20. Inga-Stina Ewbank, *Their Proper Sphere: A Study of the Brontë Sisters
as Early-Victorian Female Novelists* (Cambridge: Harvard University Press,
1966), p. 173.

fellow-creatures to say that they ought to confine themselves to making puddings and knitting stockings, to playing the piano and embroidering bags. [I, chap. 12, 110–11]

Wonderful oratory as this is, it is not merely a speech tossed into the novel. For one thing, reading it anywhere, one would know the voice: unmistakably, this is Jane Eyre. And this central consciousness gathers up here the outrage, boiling up around Charlotte Brontë in Yorkshire as she wrote these lines, of class and sex against imposed confinement of ambition and spirit.

The passions of sex and class, in their essential connection, propel the book; but the focus of passion in the novel is Jane's relationship with Rochester. The claim for sexual equality, for a passionate fulfillment, concentrates on the possibilities that that relationship uncovers. Although the drama of this relationship draws us into it as if it were the only event in the novel, the relationship must be understood in the whole context of Jane's education, her active making of her self. Before Jane leaves Lowood for Thornfield she is visited by Bessie, Mrs. Reed's servant. The point of the visit is to emphasize that Jane has finished a stage in her development; Bessie quizzes Jane about her drawing, her music, her French; Bessie betrays her admiration, compares Jane favorably with the Reed sisters.

Jane Eyre narrates her own story: we rarely see her in situations that might yield objective assessment of her achievements, power, or maturity. Bessie serves here as an objective observer: we know how far Jane has progressed. Once she leaves Lowood, however, and once she becomes immersed in her relationship with Rochester, we again lose sight of Jane's growth. She is still a young woman; her experience is limited to Lowood and Thornfield. The richness of that experience becomes clear only upon her return to Gateshead to tend her dying aunt. Upon her arrival the sisters Eliza and Georgianna greet her with their habitual superciliousness. But

a sneer, however, whether covert or open, had now no longer
that power over me it once possessed: as I sat between my
cousins, I was surprised to find how easy I felt under the total
neglect of one and the semi-sarcastic attentions of the other. . . . The fact was . . . within the last few months feelings
had been stirred in me so much more potent than any they
could raise—pains and pleasures so much more acute and ex-
quisite . . . that their airs gave me no concern either for good or
bad. [II, chap. 6, 231]

In a novel full of excitement, this passage introduces a cool,
subdued interlude; but an important one. For in an atmosphere without love or attachment, it demonstrates Jane's
(new) sureness of herself, shows us a Jane able to look with
detachment and resourcefulness at the petty lives of the Reed
sisters and the unrepentant death of their mother. Since what
Jane returns to at Thornfield is a test of strength, it is especially important that at this point we gain a clear sense of what
she has and what she has not come to know about her world
and herself. The scenes at Gateshead amply display Jane's
growing maturity.

If *Jane Eyre* registers the impact of the shaping changes of
the first decades of the nineteenth century, Jane's conflict with
Rochester exemplifies the possibilities those changes opened
out. The fullness of a mature human life is fought for in their
relationship; and the relationship illustrates well the possible
conditions, in 1847–48, of such a fullness. In the climactic
scenes with Rochester the question of self is put in relation
with the question of society in a new way. The essential
concern—What will be good for me? What will make for my
psychic well-being?—is weighed now against the real impact
of what Avrom Fleishman calls "external" limitations. The
question of "external" equality surfaces with a sudden power.
Jane and Rochester have already affirmed that they are *spiritu-
ally* equal. Although Jane does not set this affirmation aside,
she faces now the impact on Rochester and herself of the
various kinds of inequality that persist. The most obvious kind

is the inequality of money. But more fundamental is the thorough social inequality between man and woman. This feeling of inequality simmered in the brief period of courtship when Jane shifted unhappily under the burden of Rochester's gifts. Now it comes out powerfully as an impediment because, once the protection of established, legitimized relationship has been removed, Jane faces Rochester stripped to herself—that is, as a penniless, dependent *woman*. As a woman, Jane asks uneasily whether marriage or, in her case, a continuing relationship without legal sanction can truthfully be considered a private and not a social connection. At this crucial turning point in the novel Jane thus puts the novel's crucial question: Can spiritual equality be claimed and realized without the basis of social equality?

Jane leaves Rochester because her integrity is at stake; this is clear and convincing, even though what she says is at once puzzling and out of character. Rochester insists she remain with him: who would know? "'Who in the world cares for *you?* or who will be injured by what you do?'"

> "*I* care for myself. The more solitary, the more friendless, the more unsustained I am, the more I will respect myself. I will keep the law given by God; sanctioned by man. I will hold to the principles received by me when I was sane, and not mad—as I am now.... Preconceived opinions, foregone determinations, are all I have at this hour to stand by: there I plant my foot." [III, chap. 1, 321]

What preconceived opinions? Where do they come from? How has Jane come to them? The only answer the book allows is that Jane is referring to her training at Lowood: we have here the essential mediation of Miss Temple at a moment of crisis and the book's ultimate affirmation of received opinion. Value is here, as in *Mansfield Park*, "inherited." But I believe that this point of view is argued at the very juncture where it is shown to be weak and, at best, secondary. Fanny Price's principles are given to her whole by Jane Austen, but we observe her living by them; she adjusts self to custom, propriety, preconceived opinions, and foregone determinations; when circumstance confuses alternatives, she ponders choice in the language of principle. Jane, on the other hand, follows the demands of self: when circumstance confuses alternatives, she struggles to clarify her feelings, to discover what will most fully satisfy, what will most certainly make for life.[21] For the most part Jane's *principled* stands are expressions of integrity; only when she leaves Rochester does she invoke convention and received opinion.

But the conventional gesture toward society—the law given by God, sanctioned by man—at best obliquely states the real social pressure, which is the pressure generated by inequality of power. Were Jane to remain, she would be wholly in Rochester's power. Such powerlessness not only is unacceptable under the circumstances, but would have been unacceptable even under the conditions of legal marriage. Jane and Rochester's relationship, one can say, has come, in the scenes just after the abortive bigamous marriage ceremony, to that point of crisis at which it must pass from the affinities of soul to a working arrangement that will sustain those affinities; romance attained, Jane and Rochester must establish a marriage. But neither Jane nor Rochester is ready for a marriage of true equality. Jane is not strong enough to resist Rochester except by recourse to conventional pieties; she is besides poor and dependent. Rochester, though he loves Jane, expresses love to her as he would to any other woman: he wants to dress her up; and he relishes both her dependence and his overweening sexual, social, and pecuniary dominance.

Having forced herself to say farewell to Rochester, Jane dreams that she is again a child in the red room: she is again threatened by the extinction of self she suffered as a child. But now, as an adult, her ordeal is more thorough and more prolonged. Deprived of spiritual union with the man she loves,

21. See Q. D. Leavis's "Introduction" to *Jane Eyre* (Harmondsworth: Penguin Books, 1966).

she hovers on the edge of believing herself deprived of life. She comes near death, but endures partly because of her will to live and partly because she is rescued by—as it turns out— her family. That the Rivers sisters and St. John are indeed her relatives is a piece of contrivance we may judge artless; but it is thematically right and important. The soul's self-seeking, in this instance as in the incidents following Jane's collapse in the red room, turns now outward, toward a social rather than a private satisfaction.

For the first time since Lowood Jane settles into relation-ships with people of her own age, on an intellectual as well as emotional plane; she becomes active in work of some responsi-bility as a teacher; she is sustained by a round of social rela-tionships, and becomes a fixture in her neighborhood. Finally she inherits £20,000, and assumes a new role as an indepen-dent woman. We are apt to think of the incidents at Thornfield as making up the whole novel; but between Jane's break with Rochester and her return occur one hundred pages of narrative, a good part of them devoted to the detailing of Jane's enlarged experience, her new-won competence, and her increasing exercise of power. The final battle with St. John returns the book to drama, and exposes to us and to Jane what she needs and what she wants. But the intervening discovery of family, money, social routine, and power is more important in the larger purpose of the book, for it establishes Jane's social stature and allows her to look at Rochester no longer as an idol.

This is the Jane, then, who marries Rochester, a woman whose maturity we properly can emphasize as "achieved." The process of her growth has been an extraordinarily active interchange between self and experience. It must be said nonetheless that in this, the most human and profound fic-tional expression of individualism as a means to self-fulfillment, we find at the end some doubt that what the characters have gained is equality and that what individualism has found is a social embodiment.

The novel argues that spiritual equality can be realized only under the conditions of social equality, under conditions of an equality of power. Jane returns to Rochester a far more powerful woman than she left him; she finds Rochester far weaker. Does the novel take revenge on Rochester for his overweening virility and his social rank? The novel struggles to work through to equality, a struggle dramatized in Jane's life. But this equality cannot be gained merely by Jane's rise: Rochester must fall. Partly Rochester must fall from his high disdain and his utterly misguided godlike arrogance about his role as a man.[22] Jane may love but she cannot marry the Rochester who would bury her in finery and treat her as if a marriage could be made out of mere spiritual affinity, as if they could live on the moon. Marriage demands a social expression of love, a social equality as well as a spiritual one. In this respect Rochester's fall is necessary and satisfying: the house, symbol of his power and licentiousness, is properly burned, and its "bestial" inhabitant exorcized. But Rochester's blindness and his loss of one hand leave him abject and crippled. Jane relishes her job of "rehumanizing" Rochester, in effect of mastering him. The novel maintains, in its final sections, that a true balance has been regained, that each now lives for the other in a full equality. The whole impetus of the novel has been toward this place of equality, and so Jane's final words do not sound like the hollow summing up at the end of a book, a mere tying together of loose strings. But nonetheless these believable assertions do not match the fiery end of Thornfield. The energy of the novel's close is concentrated in this single event, explosive and dramatic as it must be.

The truth is that once relationships are put in terms of power, it is difficult to achieve equality.[23] It is especially dif-

22. Cf. Adrienne Rich, "*Jane Eyre:* The Temptations of a Motherless Woman," *Ms.*, October 1973.
23. Cf. Eagleton, *Myths of Power*, pp. 29–30:
Yet Jane does not finally claim equality with Rochester; the primary terms on which Charlotte Brontë's fiction handles relationships are

ficult when what must be achieved is equality between individuals who begin as far apart as do Jane and Rochester, and when it must be achieved in a society where that inequality seems only proper. And as the dynamic presence of power, wealth, class, privilege in the novel, Rochester must suffer a fall; I think we must say that the fall expresses a long-suppressed anger on Charlotte Brontë's part as well as a certain despair at not being able to imagine, or rather not to realize, conditions of true equality. Her fascination with the master-servant, teacher-pupil relationship severely qualifies her claim that Jane and Rochester achieve sexual equality.[24] So does the novel's resting place at Ferndean. The marriages between Elizabeth and Darcy and between Fanny and Edmund are social in an obvious way. Jane Austen has no difficulty in believing they are possible, or in mapping out for us in imagination the successful pattern of these characters' married lives. Her vision has a concrete social manifestation. But Jane's marriage to Rochester is more complex, and Charlotte Brontë cannot as easily imagine what social place this marriage will fill. Ferndean is cut off in its shrubbery and wildness, more like the hideout of Robin Hood than the home of a rich landowner. Jane and Rochester spend their time wholly together; there is some suggestion that Diana and Mary Rivers, both married by the end of the novel, form with their husbands what Austen would have called a family circle. Perhaps, but the relationship we are shown is the solitary one between

---

those of dominance and submission. The novels dramatize a society in which almost all human relationships are power struggles; and because "equality" therefore comes to be defined as equality of power, it is an inevitably complicated affair.... Whether she likes it or not, Jane finally comes to have power over Rochester. Her ultimate relation to him is a complete blend of independence (she comes to him on her own terms, financially self-sufficient), submissiveness, and control.

24. Ewbank makes the startling and eerie suggestion that "the teaching-situation ... not only obliterates conventional social superiority; it is also in itself an image of the ideal man-woman relationship" (*Their Proper Sphere*, p. 200).

Rochester and Jane in the forest. The novel endows Jane with a necessary social stature and asserts the practical and thus essential need for a developed social base for marriage. Yet the novel hesitates to believe that the fulfillment of self which it has traced, the fulfillment of a poor, plain woman, can actually find social expression. The novel establishes the basis for an equality in marriage but hangs back in romance, uncertain that in the society of the Reeds, the Brocklehursts, and the Ingrams such fulfillment can flourish: the transformations of self once achieved, the full transformation of society seems daunting, and the novel retreats into its overgrown paradise. This paradise serves at once as a criticism of that other, public world and as an announcement of a deep, dispiriting gulf between active self-fulfillment and social possibility.

IV

"My mother left me to my grandmother," said Bounderby; "and, according to the best of my remembrance, my grandmother was the wickedest and the worst old woman that ever lived. If I got a little pair of shoes by any chance, she would take 'em off and sell 'em for drink. . . ."

. . .

"I pulled through it, though nobody threw me out a rope. Vagabond, errand-boy, vagabond, labourer, porter, clerk, chief manager, small partner, Josiah Bounderby of Coketown."

—CHARLES DICKENS, *Hard Times*

Thus the "Bully of humility," self-made, "nobody to thank for my being here but myself" (bk. I, chap. 4, 16, 17). Dickens has wonderfully entangled this man, the agent of a major perversion of the idea of value, with the representative of an opposite but connected and similarly discredited system of feeling, the redoubtable Mrs. Sparsit. This formidable Victorian lady

had not only seen different days but was highly connected. She had a great-aunt living in these very times called Lady Scadgers. Mr. Sparsit, deceased, of whom she was the relict, had been by the mother's side what Mrs. Sparsit still called "a Powler". . . . The better class of minds . . . did not need to be informed that the Powlers were an ancient stock, who could trace themselves so exceedingly far back that it was not surprising if they sometimes lost themselves—which they had rather frequently done, as respected horse-flesh, blind-hookey, Hebrew monetary transactions, and the Insolvent Debtors' Court. [Bk. I, chap. 7, 48]

Clearly something has gone wrong by the time we get to these passages. "In these very times"—suddenly a present is acknowledged we have not previously met with, a present in which both Austen and Brontë appear, suddenly, dated. We have passed here through transition and transformation to a disenchanted arrival on the other side. The alliances by which the old system might be sustained in Austen and the activity by means of which one might find and fulfill oneself in Brontë both appear in these passages in an inverted, not to say perverted, form. The possibilities and interpretations of Austen and Brontë emerge here as *the past;* the present is history's judgment of Austen's and Brontë's possibilities.

Of course Bounderby and Mrs. Sparsit do not exactly counterbalance each other. Bounderby speaks a living, powerful, and dangerous cant; Mrs. Sparsit is a "relict." In Bounderby we find Jane Eyre's buoyant individualism gone bitter, turned against others, swelled up into a bragging oppressiveness. Bounderby's autobiographical blasts debase a liberating idea—you can make your own life—into a taunt: I was as badly off as you, and now I'm rich; if you don't have it in you to get rich, don't complain. Nothing in Mrs. Sparsit matches the real, painful thrust of such an attitude. Bounderby is the driving agent of Coketown; but in Coketown the solemnity with which Burke, Austen, and in ways even Brontë approached heritage, lineage, and blood appears merely ridiculous. If Mrs. Sparsit is now, significantly, the handmaiden of a newer pretentiousness, she has nonetheless no status of her own.

But in *Hard Times* neither Bounderby nor Mrs. Sparsit ever fills out to become a true individual, a character in his or her own right. Whatever liberties of that sort Dickens allows them, these liberties are overwhelmed by the characters' essential function as aspects of a schema. Eugene Forçade, in his 1848 review of *Jane Eyre*, wrote perceptively that "the novel is the form of poetry devoted to the individual history of human emotion."[25] This observation is true, without being limiting, of *Jane Eyre*, and true as well of *Pride and Prejudice* and *Mansfield Park*; but it is true of *Hard Times* only if we mean by "individual history" something strikingly different. In Austen and Brontë "human emotion" exists within the life of a character, embodied, sometimes concentrated, in an individual's particular attitude toward life or made emblematic by a character's "typical" history. But the connections among social and economic relations, the structure of ideology, and the pattern of individual life remain in those novels implicit, embedded in plot or form and mediated by daily life and the wholeness of character. The structure of feeling is expressed but not openly examined. Dickens writes differently:

> It was a town of red brick, or of brick that would have been red if the smoke and ashes had allowed it. . . . It was a town of machinery and tall chimneys, out of which interminable serpents of smoke trailed themselves forever and ever. . . . It contained several large streets all like one another, inhabited by people equally like one another, who all went . . . to do the same work, and to whom every day was the same as yesterday and tomorrow. . . .
>
> These attributes of Coketown were in the main inseparable from the work by which it was sustained; against them were to be set off comforts of life which found their way all over the world. . . .
>
> You saw nothing in Coketown but what was severely workful. If the members of a religious persuasion built a chapel

25. Eugene Forçade, *Revue des deux mondes*, October 31, 1848, quoted in Allott, *The Brontës*, p. 101.

there—as the members of eighteen religious persuasions had done—they made it a pious warehouse of red brick. . . . Fact, fact, fact, everywhere, in the material aspect of the town; fact, fact, fact, everywhere in the immaterial. [Bk. I, chap. 5, 24–25]

Certainly recorded here is the history of a human emotion. But the explicit relationship of material and immaterial, the explicit handling of a structure of feeling, creates new problems in the delineation of fictional character. One of Dickens's solutions is there in such figures as Bounderby and Mrs. Sparsit. They too, like Fanny and Jane, embody human emotion; but now it is virtually a single emotion. This concentration does not, however, make them into caricatures. They contain not just a single emotion, but an emotion the material and immaterial aspects of which are both made overt, and an emotion that is not strictly individual but seen to be typical and representative. These characters act out, in *Hard Times*, the history of a place and a system. Because they do so, we find in the novel special concern with the impact of circumstance on character, special because the novel's intention is overtly to make judgments about what will and what will not make for a viable human society.

Perhaps we could say that Austen had the same intention in *Mansfield Park*. But in *Mansfield Park* Austen indulged a liberty of interpretation Dickens cannot. Austen was able to write as if the system of money which the Crawfords represent and the landed values of Mansfield Park were engaged in a conflict soluble, in real terms, in favor of Mansfield. Mansfield Park not only *ought* to triumph: its triumph is seen in the novel as an actual possibility. The contradiction of ideologies in the novel is seen to be acted out before any determining decision. Now Austen writes against history; the system of money had *in fact* triumphed long before the writing of her novel; and she herself demonstrates this ascendancy in Sir Thomas's dependence on Antigua and in Tom's profligacy. Nonetheless she is able, within the structure of the novel, to criticize the dominant moneyed system of value without a sense of necessary defeat; she is able to do so because she mystifies the source of value in *Mansfield Park*, and can place her faith in the primacy of Mansfield's ideology as if that ideology were autonomous, separate from any actual material base.

Now Dickens has set himself a harder task, and indeed finds himself in a more difficult historical situation. It may have been possible, if one lived in an isolated genteel enclosure in Austen's countryside, and looked out from inside the Great House, to believe that what Cobbett saw standing in the fields outside was not fact but a matter of interpretation. But in Coketown it surely was not possible to believe that the system of industrial capitalism had not attained dominance, or so fully to ignore its tremendous material consequences. (Although one says this remembering that for such men as Ure it was, at the very least, possible to separate capitalist industry from its consequences in social life.) So that whatever Dickens may feel about the *oughts* of the matter, he begins, actually, not with a general intention to judge what will and what will not make for a viable human society but rather—and this is a tremendous qualification—what will and will not make for a viable human life *in Coketown*. And this is the ground of Dickens's greatest achievements in *Hard Times* and his greatest failures. His achievements are the consequences of his hatred for Coketown as a structure of feeling and his decisive account of this structure as growing from the material circumstances of Coketown life. But while Dickens in this way sets out to offer an analysis of what Coketown is all about, at the same time he accepts the fact that Coketown has solidly arrived, that if there are to be alternatives they must be alternatives *within* Coketown, and so his criticism is disabled from the outset. Basically Dickens accepts Coketown and tries to find solace, really, within it. His posited alternative, the circus, only superficially contradicts this. The circus is, of course, entirely

severed from the system of life in Coketown.[26] It is an en-
campment on the outside of town, a rootless social sector, a
tent that's thrown up and into which the people of Coketown
pass for some relief, but a tent that in any event comes down.
Although in terms of plot the circus appears in contradiction
to Coketown, structurally it functions as a sort of relief *within*
Coketown.

The impact of circumstance on character in *Hard Times*
differs, then, from that in Austen's novels in that circumstance
is now, on the whole, extended to include the entire complex
of social, economic, and political relations, and therefore circumstance and consequently character take on an important,
an overtly noted, ideological dimension. Here Louisa, having
run from Harthouse and (unknown to her) Mrs. Sparsit, confronts her father:

> "This minute he expects me. . . . I do not know that I am
> sorry, I do not know that I am ashamed, I do not know that I
> am degraded in my own esteem. All I know is, your philoso-
> phy and your teaching will not save me. Now, Father, you
> have brought me to this. Save me by some other means!"
> He tightened his hold in time to prevent her sinking on the
> floor. . . . And he laid her down there, and saw the pride of his
> heart and the triumph of his system lying, an insensible heap,
> at his feet. [Bk. II, chap. 12, 254]

No doubt Dickens could not resist the blunt pun on "insensible." But Louisa, who comes as close as any of the characters
to assuming a life of her own, is nevertheless always, as herself, also the triumph of Gradgrind's system. It is fitting that
she, the purported epitome of sense (not sensibility), has come
to this: to lie insensible before her father. The human drama,

---

26. Cf. Raymond Williams's discussion of *Hard Times* in *Culture and
Society, 1780–1950* (Garden City: Anchor Books, Doubleday, 1959), pp. 99–
104; and John Holloway, *"Hard Times:* A History and a Criticism," in
Dickens and the Twentieth Century, ed. John Gross and Gabriel Pearson (London: Routledge & Kegan Paul, 1962), pp. 159–74.

despite Louisa's genuinely moving sentences, barely shines through the assertion of ideology. Nor, in a sense, *can* the human drama do so, for the two are inextricably intertwined in this novel, so that without their ideological aspects the human characters have no meaning.

One could extend the list of such examples considerably; the most artful example is this one, describing the disguised Tom, in Sleary's Horse-riding:

> In a preposterous coat, like a beadle's, with cuffs and flaps exaggerated to an unspeakable extent; in an immense waistcoat, knee-breeches, buckled shoes, and a mad cocked hat; with nothing fitting him, and everything of coarse material, moth-eaten and full of holes; with seams in his black face, where fear and heat had started through the greasy composition daubed all over it—anything so grimly, detestably, ridiculously shameful as the whelp in his comic livery, Mr. Gradgrind never could by any other means have believed in, weighable and measurable fact though it was. And one of his model children had come to this!   [Bk. III, chap. 7, 328]

Tom is a child of Fact, a man without a heart. The circus is the domain of love and compassion, an attractive and graceful place. The emotional makeup of Sleary's troupers is captured in their literal makeup: their blackface, costumes, routines reflect the grace of their being. But in this gentle, forgiving world Tom is an alien, an inhuman stranger, and the garb of the circus people accentuates his own inner corruption, his inability to inhabit the privileged circle. Within the tent of Sleary's Horse-riding, Gradgrind for the first time sees his son for what he really is (and what he has made him): an ugly, grotesque pretender to humanity.

Having said this, however, one comes back to the *similarities* between Austen and Dickens. The structural basis of these similarities is the perception that circumstance makes character; for, although in *Hard Times* circumstance extends well beyond the family, yet insofar as the novel concentrates on a few characters, it too portrays, to borrow a phrase, the world of our fathers. The paternal and ideological center of the novel is the utilitarian Thomas Gradgrind, retired hardware merchant, member of Parliament, philanthropist, ideologue. Gradgrind is specifically shown as concerned centrally with the production of value: it is in the realm of education that his system is tested and judged. His educational philosophy is at once famous and perfectly straightforward: "reason is . . . the only faculty to which education should be addressed" (bk. I, chap. 4, 21). To demonstrate the efficacy of this benign and practical maxim, Gradgrind not only establishes a model school, but offers to the admiring multitude the lives of his children, raised after his own special utilitarian plan. Gradgrind's responsibility and failure are, then—though in a different key, to be sure—much like Sir Thomas Bertram's. Significantly the crisis of responsibility in *Hard Times*, as in *Mansfield Park*, involves a marriage.

> "Mr. Bounderby has made his proposal of marriage to me, and has entreated me to make it known to you, and to express his hope that you will take it unto your favorable consideration."
>
> Silence between them. The deadly statistical clock very hollow. The distant smoke very black and heavy.
>
> "Father," said Louisa, "do you think I love Mr. Bounderby?"
>
> Mr. Gradgrind was extremely discomfited by this unexpected question. [Bk. I, chap. 15, 112]

The deadly statistical clock, the heavy smoke—Gradgrind's system is as responsible for these things as it is for the marriage he now negotiates. Louisa's discomfiting question unsettles him only for a moment; he decides she has used a "misplaced" expression, and should confine herself to Fact:

> "Confining yourself rigidly to Fact, the question of Fact you state to yourself is: Does Mr. Bounderby ask me to marry him? Yes, he does. The sole remaining question then is: Shall I marry him? I think nothing can be plainer than that?"

"Shall I marry him?" repeated Louisa, with great delibera-
tion.
                    . . .
From the beginning, she had sat looking at him fixedly. As
he now leaned back in his chair, and bent his deep-set eyes
upon her in his turn, perhaps he might have seen one wavering
moment in her, when she was impelled to throw herself upon
his breast, and give him the pent-up confidences of her heart.
But, to see it, he must have overleaped . . . the artificial bar-
riers he had for many years been erecting between himself and
all those subtle essences of humanity. . . .
Removing her eyes from him, she sat so long looking silently
towards the town that he said at length: "Are you consulting
the chimneys of the Coketown works, Louisa?"
"There seems to be nothing there but languid and monoto-
nous smoke. Yet when night comes, Fire bursts out, Father!"
she answered, turning quickly.   [Bk. I, chap. 15, 114–15]

The essential irresponsibility here does not much distinguish
Gradgrind from Sir Thomas, although their daughters are
very different, products of very different systems, and they
make very different decisions. But the final stroke, the introduction of the smokestacks and Louisa's charged observation,
places the passage beyond Jane Austen. The interaction of
material and immaterial is here brilliantly displayed.

We have already seen the consequences, material and immaterial, of Gradgrind's system, insofar as they pertain to
Louisa. Abandoned into a grotesque marriage, exploited by
her corrupted brother, Louisa finally collapses under the emotional demands of the conventionally dashing James Harthouse. Her brother Tom, once let out of the arithmetical closet
at Stone Lodge, follows very much the path of Tom Bertram,
though for other reasons. From gambling he falls, as Austen
could not allow Tom Bertram to do, to robbery, and then to
ruin and finally death in a foreign country. Dickens's judgment of Gradgrind is, as this progression makes clear, far
more severe than Austen's judgment of Sir Thomas. The
whole energy of *Mansfield Park* is invested in the reclamation
of Sir Thomas's failed ventures, including especially his chil-

dren. But Dickens does not believe Coketown can be reclaimed; Tom dies and Louisa is condemned to a life without a full emotional flowering.

Circumstance, then, takes on a grim aspect in Dickens; and not only is circumstance inherently destructive, but its hold on the individual is firmer and somehow more thorough than in Austen. This is to say that in *Hard Times* there is not the slightest possibility that one could, by one's own effort, make one's life. The possibilities of personal transformation do not exist. This reality is bitter and despairing, but disguised in the novel by a number of factors. The first is that Dickens shows that if deadly circumstances make for various kinds of emotional death, beneficent circumstances make for emotional vitality. The prime example is of course Sissy Jupe. Born into the circus and inculcated with the generous ethic of Sleary and her father, Sissy can neither quite grasp what Gradgrind is about—she confuses National Prosperity with Natural Prosperity—nor become recast by Gradgrind's system; he has got to her, the novel says, too late. It is by means of Sissy that the ideological opposite to Fact gets introduced into the novel; Sissy refuses to believe that her father will not reappear. When Gradgrind regularly answers her inquiries by telling her he has heard nothing,

> the trembling of Sissy's lip would be repeated in Louisa's face, and her eyes would follow Sissy with compassion to the door. Mr. Gradgrind usually improved on these occasions by remarking, when she was gone, that if Jupe had been properly trained from an early age she would have remonstrated to herself on sound principles the baselessness of these fantastic hopes. Yet it did seem (though not to him, for he saw nothing of it) as if fantastic hope could take as strong a hold as Fact. [Bk. I, chap. 9, 71]

Sissy performs an honorable role in the novel, sentimentalized as she is. She lives in Stone Lodge as a being of flesh and blood; she becomes the strength of the house when it falls into its emotional crisis upon Louisa's return; and she palliates Gradgrind's harsh regime to the extent that the younger Gradgrinds evince real signs of common humanity. For all that, one perceives uneasily the contrast between fantastic hope and Fact; this is an early sign of the novel's deep structural flaws.

So long as the novel focuses on the Gradgrind family, the system of Fact coheres and the central, determining conviction that circumstance makes character holds. And within the Gradgrind household Sissy does maintain a vital, oppositional ideology. But the material sources of Fact and fanciful hope are so badly inapposite that even within Stone Lodge they seem less to contradict each other than to be irrelevant to each other. The system of Fact, after all, pervades Coketown life, emanates from its centers of production, at once expresses the mode of production and shapes it; Fact is the basis of bank, factory, Parliament, and home. Can Dickens seriously pit the circus against all that? What does the circus really have to do with Coketown?

Dicken's final answer to this question occurs at the opening of the chapter that introduces Stephen Blackpool. "I entertain a weak idea that the English people are as hard-worked as any people upon whom the sun shines. I acknowledge to this ridiculous idiosyncrasy as a reason why I would give them a little more play" (bk. I, chap. 10, 72). Is this what *Hard Times* boils down to? Insofar as the opposition of Fact and Fancy go, I believe it is. People must be amused, as Sleary says. That is Dicken's final observation on Coketown. How it comes to be so is clear in the chapter that follows the passage above.

Stephen Blackpool is that embarrassing figure, the good workman. In a novel where everything else is typical, he is fobbed off on us as that other, more important figure, the representative workman, the epitome of, in Dickens's words, "the hardest working part of Coketown" (bk. I, chap. 10, 72). A bent, thin, grey, worn individual, Stephen is dubbed Old Stephen; he has known, we are told, "a peck of trouble." It turns out, however, that he's not old at all but prematurely grey from the hard life imposed on him—not by the system of

Fact, by industrial capitalism and mechanization, but by his drunken wife. If it were not for his drunken wife, whom Stephen can't ever be fully rid of because he can't get a divorce, Stephen would marry his friend Rachel and be perfectly happy.

> No word of a new marriage had ever passed between them; but . . . he knew very well that if he were free to ask her, she would take him. He thought of the home he might at that moment have been seeking with pleasure and pride; of the different man he might have been that night; of the lightness in his now heavy-laden breast. . . . He thought of the waste of the best part of his life . . . of the dreadful nature of his existence, bound hand and foot, to a dead woman, and tormented by a demon in her shape. [Bk. I, chap. 12, 93]

We are asked to see Stephen as the victim of circumstance: his life is subject to the defining pressures of Coketown life at its most basic, at the levels of work and class. He is the victim of circumstances that we see elsewhere as relentlessly destructive of people's lives. But the idea that Stephen is a victim of circumstance is initially contradicted by the source of his woes, which is at best peripheral to the system of Fact, and which, once removed, leaves the idea that circumstance had made his character a very doubtful proposition. The passage above explicitly maintains that free of his drunken wife, Stephen would be a "different man." Yet, insofar as Stephen is like all the other workers, nothing would have changed. What then of the idea that circumstance makes character?

This idea is undermined in the novel with equal force in the case of Bounderby. "'Josiah in the gutter!' exclaimed Mrs. Pegler. 'No such a thing, sir. Never! For shame on you! My dear boy knows . . . that though he come of humble parents, he come of parents that loved him as dear as the best could, and never thought it hardship on themselves to pinch a bit that he might write and cipher beautiful . . .'" (bk. III, chap. 5, 302–3). Which is to say the vilest character in the novel, the Bully of humility, was in fact the son of loving parents, and was raised in a home devoted to his care. What then of Dickens's criticism of Gradgrind's system as empty of emotion? Here is a man raised in a home Sissy Jupe herself would have to admire who has yet grown into a heartless, pitiless adult; an adult, moreover, who reigns as the powerful center of Coketown, as banker and industrialist.

F. R. Leavis, in a phrase that has entered all subsequent criticism of *Hard Times*, wrote that the book displays a "comprehensive vision."[27] The phrase, surely, does not stand by itself; it is not self-evident. The passages about Stephen and Bounderby indicate why it is not. Partly, at the very level where the book makes its claims—in ideology—it is contradictory. Partly, once actually into the working life of Coketown, Dickens goes somehow badly astray, establishes for Stephen a material dilemma that is strictly arbitrary. Dickens refuses to portray Stephen's real life, preferring to pit this Stephen against the workers as a whole society, to picture him as a lone outsider in a startlingly contemporary alienation: "Thus easily did Stephen Blackpool fall into the loneliest of lives, the life of solitude among a familiar crowd" (bk. II, chap. 4, 167).

At the heart of these contradictions I think one finds a crisis specifically related to energy. Insofar as Dickens portrays Coketown as a structure of feeling, what we experience is the extraordinary power of circumstance over human life, of Fact and factory over the human spirit. The lives of the characters most directly subject to such determination, the lives of the characters with whom we most sympathize—Louisa and Stephen—are cursed by a crushing monotony and deadness of feeling. Coketown is all smoke and no fire. And yet this hard, grey, dismal world is detailed in a language of wonderful inventiveness, energy, and zest for life. This is Jane Eyre's mak-

27. F. R. Leavis, *The Great Tradition* (Harmondsworth: Penguin Books, 1962 [1948]), p. 250. The notion of the novel as more philosophical than Dickens's others, and more focused, has been subsequently argued by, for instance, Edgar Johnson, *Charles Dickens: His Tragedy and Triumph* (Boston: Little, Brown, 1952), II, 801–19; and Philip Collins, *Dickens and Education* (London: Macmillan, 1963), pp. 144–46.

ing activity become the language of creation. If there is comprehensiveness in the novel it is here, for Dickens's language itself defines the human impulse that abominates Coketown as a system.[28]

But against this linguistic inventiveness must be placed the impossibility of energy, especially of a transforming energy, in the lives and institutions that the novel depicts. For Jane Austen the idea that circumstance makes character represented a viable means of ensuring the reproduction of inherited value. It was by no means a dark or despairing insight. But for Dickens the idea becomes a kind of signal for doom. Where he comes close, in his novel, to situations in which characters might themselves change circumstances, he either presents the possibility of change as a form of personal tyranny, as with Bounderby, or as a broader class tyranny, as with the trades union. The final statement becomes then his title to Chapter 11: "No Way Out."

No way out—except that the very words are part of a new vitality, a living, thriving, urban structure of feeling, and so indicate a way out already in the making. But this is a structure of feeling in which some observations are clearer than others, in which some feelings contradict others, in which comprehensiveness means a single, sustained sense of the quality of urban life rather than comprehensiveness of response, analysis, or understanding. Finally this is a vital structure in which Charlotte Brontë's distinction between political and other kinds of rebellion has become, if anything, more power-

28. Cf. F. R. Leavis and Q. D. Leavis, *Dickens the Novelist* (New York: Random House, 1970), in which F. R. Leavis writes of *Hard Times* (p. 194): "To the question how the reconciling is done . . . the answer can be given by pointing to the astonishing and irresistible richness of life that characterizes the book everywhere. It meets us everywhere, unrestrained and natural, in the prose. Out of such prose a great variety of presentations can arise congenially with equal vividness. There they are, unquestionably 'real.' It goes back to an extraordinary energy of perception and registration in Dickens." I see the energy, but am less happy than Leavis that it should be concentrated so much in the prose and so little in the vision and structure.

ful. So that the author in a sense monopolizes the making of a life but forbids it in his characters; or the author fails to see a viable social agency for his own pervasive attitude, and in style and structure separates one kind of revolt from another. One comes to see, in the end, that whereas Dickens marks a definitive break with Austen and Brontë, he at the same time turns out to embody, as well, a new transition and a new set of irresolutions that must await a new historical development. The potential of a liberating direction in that development is there, in the structure and the style, but also powerfully there are the entrenched institutions of Fact and the confusions in response which might allow this contradictory vitality simply to muddle on.

CHAPTER FOUR

History and the Novel, and the Novel as History

I have tried to demonstrate correspondences between some basic elements of English social thought during the century of industrialization and some basic elements of English fiction. I have focused on the preoccupation, in classical economics in particular, with the sources and the production of value as they are expressed by various attitudes, in the fiction, toward the creation of the self. But if in *Sandford and Merton* the implications of Adam Smith's notion of value are directly applied in educational theory, the same cannot be said of *Pride and Prejudice* and *Jane Eyre*. Totally immersed in the life of the times, these novels show us the society but not necessarily the novelist in the conscious act of historical reflection. In this chapter I look at *Mansfield Park* and *Shirley* as historical novels. If in *Pride and Prejudice* and *Jane Eyre* ideology is implicit and society, as a structure, suggested but not directly portrayed, in *Mansfield Park* and *Shirley* ideology is overt and the society is assessed as a historical phenomenon, its history interpreted, and a prescription made for its continued vitality.

I *Mansfield Park*

The years between 1811 and 1813 were as turbulent and explosive as any during the first half of the nineteenth century.

By the summer of 1812 more troops were stationed in the northern counties to contain Luddism than Wellington commanded against Napoleon on the Iberian Peninsula. In May the prime minister, Spencer Perceval, was assassinated in the House of Commons, an event that caused rejoicing among rebellious workers across the nation. Factory owners were also attacked in the West Riding, and one, William Horsfall, was killed. The prince regent received threatening letters and in the North placards were put up offering 100 guineas for his head.[1]

It was at this time that Jane Austen wrote her classic defense of the landed gentry, *Mansfield Park*. This is her most historical novel, in the sense that it speaks directly about social questions and in the sense that it works to establish an *account* of a particular system, roughly the landed system in the southern counties. The novel articulates the structures of meaning of the world she regularly depicts, but more fully, more consciously, in a more systematic and calculated way than elsewhere. The most important and most perplexing historical fact of the novel is that the estate of Sir Thomas Bertram depends on a sugar plantation in the West Indian island of Antigua. Avrom Fleishman has enumerated the questions that this dependence raises: "What are we to make of the fact that Mansfield is not a self-sufficient estate, that the family's way of life is threatened, and that the large and airy rooms depend on an external and troubled colonial holding for their support? And if a question about offstage action may be admitted, what does Sir Thomas *do* in Antigua to make secure the sources of his income?"[2] These are important questions. They are important for our understanding of the novel; but, as well, they are important because the novel takes the estate of Sir Thomas to be representative of those of his class, and because the novel

1. See E. P. Thompson, *The Making of the English Working Class* (Harmondsworth: Penguin Books, 1968), pp. 622–24.

2. Avrom Fleishman, *A Reading of "Mansfield Park"* (Baltimore: Johns Hopkins Press, 1970), p. 36.

takes as its task the judgment and valuation of the life of that class during the decades of counterrevolution in England. The crucial dependence of Mansfield on Antigua is not a mere detail of plot but a key statement of social relationship; it touches on what for Austen as for Sir Thomas is paramount: income.

Horace Walpole, writing to Horace Mann on March 3, 1761, complained of the rising cost of buying into Parliament, for "West Indians, conquerors, nabobs, and admirals, attack every borough. . . . Venality is grosser than ever. . . . We have been as victorious as the Romans and are as corrupt."[3] Lewis Namier suggests Walpole was indulging in hyperbole, and that the cost and corruption were much the same as ever.[4] But beyond the corruption, we notice the infusion of money and the strange list Walpole makes, pointing not, as in the next century, to a development essentially within England—that is, industrial capitalism—but to developments outside England. England has become, for Walpole, another Roman Empire; it has conquered in the Caribbean and in the Indian Ocean; and the adventurers to distant places, West Indians, nabobs, admirals, have returned with their spoils to assume the power of riches. At the time Walpole wrote, the most lucrative locale of empire was the West Indies. "The world of 17th and 18th century mercantilism witnessed the rise of the Caribbean sugar industry as the chief source of new wealth. Indeed, cane sugar was probably the most valuable commodity in all the world's trade of the 18th century."[5]

Sugar was introduced to Europe on some scale as early as the fifteenth century, when Madeira, for instance, made Lisbon a great market for trade in that product;[6] but the phenom-

3. Quoted in Lewis Namier, *The Structure of Politics at the Accession of George III* (2d ed.; London: Macmillan, 1968), p. 158.
4. Ibid.
5. Richard B. Sheridan, *Sugar and Slavery: An Economic History of the British West Indies, 1623–1775* (Baltimore: Johns Hopkins Press, 1973), p. 11.
6. H. V. Livermore, *A New History of Portugal* (London: Cambridge University Press, 1966), p. 136.

enal rise in sugar use came in the next century, accompanied by a shift of production to Brazil and the West Indies, and then culminating in the massive trade in sugar and the creation of huge fortunes in the years closer to the Industrial Revolution. West Indians were identified as a specific group, separate from established power and fortune; yet as Namier himself points out, "there were comparatively few big merchants in Great Britain in 1761 who, in one connection or other, did not trade with the West Indies, and a considerable number of gentry families had interests in the Sugar Islands."[7] By 1776 about sixty members of Parliament were either West Indians themselves or intimately bound by family or property with the islands. Hampshire and Wiltshire were, by the middle of the eighteenth century, political strongholds of the West Indians.[8] Each of the islands, moreover, had its representatives not only in Parliament but in the City and in society as well. One of the means by which these interests were secured was marriage:

> Sir George Colebrooke, 2nd. Bart., M. P. for Arundel, was a London banker and chairman of the East India Company. In 1754, he married Mary Gaynor, an Antigua heiress, by whom he came into possession of three sugar estates. Similarly, Sir James Laroche, 1st. Bart., M. P. for Bodwin, and a Bristol–West India merchant, married Elizabeth Anne Yeamans, an Antigua heiress. Finally, Antigua-born Samuel Martin, son of Colonel Samuel Martin, a leading planter, was M. P. for Camelford and Hastings, Secretary to the Treasury Board, and Treasurer to the Princess Dowager of Wales.[9]

The prominence of these men exposes the power of the colonies in the shaping of English life. If there was some resentment and dismay, as on the part of Walpole in 1761 and of Cobbett later, the pervasive reality was of an England, quite small in itself, surrounded on all sides by sources of tre-

---

7. Namier, *Structure of Politics*, pp. 170–71.
8. Sheridan, *Sugar and Slavery*, pp. 60–61.
9. Ibid., p. 63.

mendous wealth that it was exploiting, and of the impact of this wealth over two centuries on the structure of power in the mother country. Of course we expect the relationship between colony and commerce; but the actual relationship was between the colonies and the whole ruling class, particularly the landed gentry. This relationship developed partly as a direct consequence of the purchase by prominent landed families of sugar estates, partly because, once fortunes had been made, planters more and more abandoned the West Indies for England. Once back, "the planters' fondest wish was to acquire an estate, blend with the aristocracy, and remove the marks of their origin."[10] And finally, when an abrupt severance was not made, the pattern of absentee ownership prevailed. The planter would spend little time on his estate; his children would be raised in England; his younger sons, cut off from the inheritance, would never visit the plantation at all. When inheritance did fall to younger sons, of course they would not change their pattern of life. So increasingly the plantations became mere sources of income as the owners blended into the life of the ruling class.[11] This relationship was so marked that Chatham declared "he should ever consider the sugar colonies as the landed interest of this kingdom, and it was barbarism to consider them otherwise."[12]

The literary image of the landed estate suffers from this account, as do other versions of the landed system as in effect anticapitalist. Income from the colonies mixed thoroughly with both commercial income and landed income. And income from the colonies was purely capitalist. As L. J. Ragatz, the most prominent historian of the British West Indies, says, the islands were developed simply for exploitation. "No considerable body of persons inspired by motives higher than the

10. Eric Williams, *Capitalism and Slavery* (New York: Russell & Russell, 1961 [1944]), p. 86.

11. See Lowell Joseph Ragatz, *Absentee Landlordism in the British Caribbean, 1750–1833* (London: Bryan Edwards Press [1929?]).

12. Quoted in Williams, *Capitalism and Slavery*, p. 95.

desire to extract the greatest possible amount of wealth from them in the shortest possible time ever reached the smiling shores of the Caribbean colonies." Consequently "planting in British territory . . . tended to be a capitalistic undertaking."[13] Moreover, a recent economic history of the British West Indies argues that "the improving landlords of 18th century England and Scotland derived their wealth from colonial property, mineral rights, and urban rents rather than from the profits of agriculture."[14] So what we find is not the landed system of Mansfield Park in its isolation, stolidly a heritage from some ancient time, but very much an integral aspect of eighteenth- and early-nineteenth-century British capitalism.

The system of commercial capitalism in the British West Indies was built on monopoly and slavery. Monopoly guaranteed the sugar planters a certain market at inflated prices in Britain, and slavery guaranteed them an unlimited supply of cheap labor. The particular brutality of slavery in the West Indies lay in the fact that slaves, once imported from Africa, would be literally used up, without much attention to their care, and then simply replaced by fresh ones brought over by ships originating in Liverpool and Bristol. The population of West Indian–born slaves never became substantial until the movement for the abolition of the slave trade took powerful form.

The source of the opposition to the slave trade and slavery was also the source of the opposition to monopoly: the industrial capitalists and free traders of Manchester. The irony of this development was that a substantial part of the capital necessary for industrial invention and production came from the huge surpluses of West Indian money that had gone into banks and investments in England.[15] Eric Williams, in his *Slavery and Capitalism*, draws the conclusion of this argument: "The commercial capitalism of the eighteenth century de-

13. Lowell Joseph Ragatz, *The Fall of the Planter Class in the British Caribbean, 1763–1833* (New York: Octagon Books, 1963 [1928]), p. 3.

14. Sheridan, *Sugar and Slavery*, p. 474.

15. Williams, *Capitalism and Slavery*, pp. 52, 96–155 *passim*.

veloped the wealth of Europe by means of slavery and monopoly. But in so doing it helped to create the industrial capitalism of the nineteenth century, which turned round and destroyed the power of commercial capitalism, slavery, and all its work."[16]

At the time in which the main action of *Mansfield Park* is set, approximately 1805–10,[17] the general decline of the British West Indies had entered a critical phase. Already in 1799 the government of Antigua had become insolvent because drought and a fall in sugar prices resulted in the inability of planters to pay their taxes. As the war with France continued, the recovery from 1799 became difficult to sustain. Partly the colonies remained solvent by pursuing an illegal trade with the United States, but Britain forbade this trade in 1805–6. Thus, cut off from the European markets by Napoleon's Continental System and from the United States by the home government, suffering from a drought in 1805 which reduced production to one-third of the average output, planters in Antigua floundered. Ragatz quotes from Governor Lavington of Antigua, writing in 1805: "'Bankruptcy is universal, and it is not confined to the Public Treasury, but extends to the Generality of Individuals resident in the Colony.'"[18] Further, by 1805 the campaign against the slave trade had assumed very serious proportions, and in 1807 Parliament voted to abolish the slave trade altogether. It is at this time of crisis that Sir Thomas travels to Antigua.

Avrom Fleishman suggests that once on his plantation, Sir Thomas

> might have sought to diversify the prevailing one-crop agriculture, which had . . . [exhausted] the soil, and then made the depression worse for the islands because they were totally de-

16. Ibid., p. 210.

17. The novel begins by looking back about thirty years and working toward the date of its action by various specific allusions (e.g., that Fanny came to Mansfield when she was ten). Given that *Mansfield Park* was begun in 1811 and published in 1814, Sir Thomas's trip to Antigua must have taken place about 1805.

18. Ragatz, *Fall of the Planter Class*, p. 306.

pendent on the largely European sugar trade, now lost. This possibility is lent credence by the fact that, as an absentee landlord, Sir Thomas would have been an exception on Antigua, which had prospered more than the neighboring islands, where absentee ownership was the rule. A vigorous estate owner would have had to be present to make the large-scale planting decisions required precisely at this critical time.[19]

All of these suggestions are groundless. As one of England's first West Indian colonies, Antigua suffered early from problems of soil depletion coupled with damage from droughts. It was therefore, of all the islands, the one most consciously devoted to agricultural innovation; by the time Sir Thomas visited Antigua, around 1805, the problem of soil depletion would have long since been dealt with on his plantation as a matter of course and island custom.[20] Even if it had been possible to begin large-scale production of other crops, the essential problems of drought, increasing competition from non-British colonies, and especially Napoleon's Continental System would not have been alleviated. There were no major markets for West Indian products but Europe and the United States. Nor is it true that Sir Thomas, as an absentee landlord, would have been an exception on Antigua. Despite the prominent example of Colonel Samuel Martin, the best-known and most vigorous of Antiguan and West Indian resident planters, Antigua essentially followed the pattern of the other colonies. A study of the sixty-five leading planter families at the middle of the eighteenth century shows that at least fifty-two were absent from the island for protracted periods. Absenteeism, too, seemed to be on the increase through the eighteenth century. Samuel Martin "not only complained of the many services he was asked to perform for absentees, but on two occasions when he went to North America and England for short visits he was perplexed to know what to do with his own estate because of the scarcity of capable plantation attorneys."[21]

19. Fleishman, *Reading of "Mansfield Park,"* p. 37.
20. Ragatz, *Fall of the Planter Class,* pp. 66–67.
21. Sheridan, *Sugar and Slavery,* p. 206.

Rather than having to go to Antigua to make major planting decisions, as Fleishman suggests, Sir Thomas was far more likely to have had to return because of the unreliability of his plantation attorneys. Historians of the West Indies are unanimous in their judgment of the disastrous consequences of absenteeism. Not only the owners were absent; often the managers in whose hands the estates were left resided elsewhere too, leaving the estates in the care of overseers.[22] In 1805 Sir Thomas would have gone to Antigua to take matters into his own hands because the extent of the crisis might have been alleviated were the fraud and mismanagement typical of overseers themselves alleviated.

Fleishman's further suggestion that Sir Thomas would have seen to it at this time that his slaves were better treated seems much more certain. Sir Thomas would have had to do so, no matter what his sentiments, because by 1805 the end of the slave trade was in sight. Survival therefore necessitated a more humane regime. But it is one thing to make this assertion and another to take it where Fleishman does.

> He goes to Antigua as a planter, presumably opposed to abolition; he occupies himself, for economic reasons, with improving the slaves' condition; he acquires some of the humanitarian or religious message of the Evangelical and other missionaries laboring in the same vineyard; and he returns critical of his own moral realm, with a warmer feeling for his young dependent, a sterner rejection of aristocratic entertainment . . . and a stronger defense of his son's dedication to resident pastoral duty.[23]

There is no warrant for this speculation. We have no evidence whatever that Sir Thomas ran into any missionaries, or that they impressed him. We have no evidence that he returned critical of his own moral realm—all suggestions in the novel are that when Sir Thomas comes home, everything goes back to normal. We may speculate that his feelings for Fanny

22. Ragatz, *Absentee Landlordism*, pp. 17–19.
23. Fleishman, *Reading of "Mansfield Park,"* p. 39.

changed while he was away, but we see the sources for his change of feeling in her behavior upon his return. Sir Thomas may have come to dislike aristocratic entertainment while he was away, but we know that Edmund believed from the start that his father would object to the theatrical. Once Sir Thomas returns and burns the copies of the play, everyone immediately accepts his behavior as entirely in character.

Fleishman tries to portray Sir Thomas as an exception to his class and to show his experiences in Antigua as especially exceptional. It seems to me sounder to argue the reverse. For I do not think it makes much sense to maintain, as Fleishman does, that the meaning of Mansfield's dependence on Antigua is revealed in Sir Thomas's new humanitarianism, or to say that this humanitarianism amounts to a representative change of heart among the gentry in a time of crisis and change.[24] Not the least objection one makes to such a point of view is that Sir Thomas's new humanitarianism is hard to find. Fleishman himself is forced to admit that it in no way directs his judgment of the marriage between Rushworth and Maria or the proposed marriage between Henry Crawford and Fanny. And while Fanny may have been opposed to slavery—she quotes from the first book of Cowper's "The Task," and we may assume she read his stanzas against slavery in the second—we have no evidence that Sir Thomas himself was opposed to it. If he did undergo such a profound change of heart, wouldn't Austen have told us so? For Sir Thomas's wealth, and consequently the whole of his way of life, depend on slavery. Had

24. Ibid. Cf. Sheridan, who writes (*Sugar and Slavery*, p. 485) that when Mr. Justice Mansfield declared in his 1772 decision that there was no basis for slavery in English law, "Samuel Martin, then living in Ashstead, Surrey, wrote to his son in London [Samuel Martin, Jr., M.P.] that the decision influenced the behavior of his servants: 'You cannot conceive, what a pitch of Insolence they are arrived at: and I fear, the many foolish Writers who are become their Advocates, will put into the heads of our Colony-negroes, to rebel; and occasion at best much blood-shed.'" Martin was the leading planter of Antigua: why should we not suppose that Sir Thomas's reactions would have been roughly like his?

he become suddenly opposed both to the slave trade and to
slavery, would this change not have caused a crisis Austen
would have had to develop? Certainly his class remained solidly behind both the trade and slavery itself; can we imagine
Sir Thomas as a crusader?

We come back, then, to Fleishman's important question:
"What are we to make of the fact that Mansfield is not a
self-sufficient estate?" The essential answer, I believe, lies in
the relation of the colonies to Britain and to the gentry in
particular. In his *Sugar and Slavery*, Richard B. Sheridan argues "that the economic growth of Great Britain was chiefly
from without inwards, that the Atlantic was the most dynamic
trading area, and that, outside of the metropolis, the most
important element in the growth of this area in the century or
more prior to 1776 was the slave-plantation, chiefly of the
cane-sugar variety in the islands of the Caribbean sea."[25]

It has somehow become possible to say of Jane Austen that
she cannot imagine meaning outside of society and at the same
time that she portrays a merely static, unchangeable society
and reveals little interest in history.[26] The truth is that, like
any other careful social observer, she sees society very clearly
in motion. If she takes the point of view of daily life, and
displays the slow accumulation of detail in that life to explosive meaning, the explosions in her books indicate always, too,
fundamental social relationships and very large facts of economic life. The significant fact of *Pride and Prejudice* is that the
Bennet estate is entailed; of *Mansfield Park* that income depends on Antigua; of *Persuasion* that estates can be lost and
that wars create riches.

Of course what Jane Austen sees clearly, even meticulously,
and what she unerringly translates into action in her novels, is
not always what she approves. Her great novels depict a

25. Sheridan, *Sugar and Slavery*, p. 475.
26. See, for example, Dorothy Van Ghent, *The English Novel* (New York:
Harper & Row, 1961 [1953]), p. 103.

threatened world.[27] And the threat is not private, a particular attack by one individual on another, but fundamentally social. Mansfield Park suffers depletion because of a failure of stewardship; but the forces that threaten Mansfield Park are the impersonal forces of history: war, the collapse of the mercantile system, money. The extraordinary expressiveness of *Mansfield Park* stems directly from its total display of the condition of the landed gentry during the years of Napoleon and Sidmouth. The connection between the gentry and the empire is essential, and historically specific. Antigua is at once the source of Sir Thomas's stature and way of life and the threat to their maintenance. Sir Thomas's struggle to preserve his social rank and the fullness of his way of life is a historical struggle; he is a historical actor, among others. And the novel gives us the historical difficulty complete, as the basis of the action.

But *Mansfield Park* is not only a display of social conditions; it is also a defense of the estate of Sir Thomas as an *idea*, and as such it is a book centrally involved in the writing of a central history: the history of the *idea* of the landed system. It is therefore a novel dedicated to a social memory, and perhaps for this reason memory plays an important part in its drama. Here we find Fanny and her half-friend Mary Crawford in the Grants' shrubbery:

> "This is pretty—very pretty," said Fanny, looking around her as they were thus sitting together one day: "Every time I come into this shrubbery I am more struck with its growth and beauty. Three years ago, this was nothing but a rough hedgerow along the upper side of the field, never thought of as any thing, or capable of becoming any thing; and now it is converted into a walk, and it would be difficult to say whether most valuable as a convenience or an ornament; and perhaps in another three years we may be forgetting—almost forgetting

27. Cf. Mary Lascelles, *Jane Austen and Her Art* (London: Oxford University Press, 1939), p. 198: "There was 'shape in the world' in which Jane Austen wrote—the firm contours of a society which to our eyes appears taut in resistance to threatened or impending change; but none of her contemporaries has her power to make us discern it."

what it was before. How wonderful, how very wonderful the
operations of time, and the changes of the human mind!" And
following the latter train of thought, she soon afterwards
added: "If any one faculty of our nature may be called *more*
wonderful than the rest, I do think it is memory. There seems
something more speakingly incomprehensible in the powers,
the failures, the inequalities of memory than in any other of
our intelligences. The memory is sometimes so retentive, so
serviceable, so obedient—at others, so bewildered and so
weak—and at others again, so tyrannic, so beyond
controul!—We are to be sure a miracle every way—but our
powers of recollecting and of forgetting, do seem peculiarly
past finding out." [Oxford edn., II, chap. 4, 208-9; Austen's
italics]

Fanny, usually reticent, withdrawn, ventures in this passage
into a major statement. The growth of this shrubbery, its
conversion from a hedgerow to a walk, contrasts with drastic
notions of improvement elsewhere in the novel. This change
has been natural, a real improvement; although even here the
improvement is the addition of a walk, an improvement for
pleasure rather than of agricultural or social benefit. Already
we have a sense, before moving to the main statement about
memory, of what will be remembered and what will be forgotten. Nonetheless, Fanny's uncharacteristic discourse on memory can be taken as a key to the reading of the novel. One
could say *Mansfield Park* is about "the powers, the failures, the
inequalities of memory."

Fanny must never forget who she is: she must remember
her place. When, Maria and Julia being away, Fanny is led by
Crawford to the head of the dance, "she could hardly believe
it. To be placed above so many elegant young women! The
distinction was too great. It was treating her like her cousins!
And her thoughts flew to those absent cousins with most un-
feigned and truly tender regret. . ." (II, chap. 10, 275-76)
Away from Portsmouth, Fanny remembers her brother
William. She is touched when others remember him. For this
reason "the recollection of what had been done for William

was always the most powerful disturber of every decision against Mr. Crawford" (III, chap. 5, 364). But Fanny is usually forgotten. Even Edmund, when Mary appears, forgets to save his mare for Fanny's exercise. When Sir Thomas is away in Antigua the family forgets what is due to him in the incident of the theatrical. Fanny wants to see Sotherton so she can keep its memory once it has been transformed by improvement.

One could extend this list to include all the major incidents in the novel. And as one uncovers more and more examples of the power or failure of memory, one becomes increasingly aware that the book is structured around absences. When Sir Thomas is absent from Mansfield, the moral worth of its inhabitants is tested by reference to how well they remember him. It is one of the criticisms of Henry Crawford that he can for so long be absent from his estate without remembering his duty to it. Fanny is shipped off to Portsmouth so that she will all the better remember both who she is and what Mansfield and wealth are. And beyond and beneath the absences of people are absences of a larger kind of theme and structure, especially the absent source of income in Antigua. What must be remembered, who must be remembered, who remembers and who forgets—these are the structures within which the novel renders moral judgment.

The method the novel employs to defend a threatened standard of value parallels the social and ideological strategy of the West Indian planters. Although Sir Thomas's source of income in Antigua is noted, the novel succeeds—to use Ragatz's formulation—in blending Sir Thomas with the aristocracy and in removing the marks of his origin. Like Chatham, Jane Austen identifies the sugar colonies with the landed interest of the kingdom. But to do so she is forced, as were the planters themselves, to obscure and distort the real nature of the dependence on Antigua and its implications. For this reason the novel sets the origin of Mansfield's value well back in a past we know nothing of, much as the West Indian planters, once established on English estates, were happy to claim an origin necessarily obscure. The historical development from this obscure past to the present of Mansfield in the early nineteenth century also remains altogether veiled. Austen invokes memory so that tradition can be validated, yet she activates memory with a careful selectiveness so that the failures of the present will not overwhelm tradition. Consequently she makes us pay attention to the estate as a "cultural space" but keeps the connection to Antigua out of sight. When Sir Thomas is away in Antigua the novel urges that we remember him and what he stands for; but when he is present the novel asks that we forget, by way of forgiveness, the failures of his stewardship. The novel's defense of a conservative structure of feeling is managed, then, by means of subtle emphasis and a selective use of memory.

We can see this in that odd turn in the novel when Henry Crawford sets out to ease Fanny's wholesale neglect at Mansfield:

> "Yes, Mary, my Fanny will feel a difference indeed . . . in the behavior of every being who approaches her. . . . Now she is dependent, helpless, friendless, neglected, forgotten."
> "Nay, Henry, not by all, not forgotten by all, not friendless or forgotten. Her cousin Edmund never forgets her." [II, chap. 12, 297]

This is a very critical statement of Fanny's situation. At this point both Henry and Mary see Fanny's role at Mansfield from her point of view. As outsiders, they confirm what we have already observed, and damn Mansfield by the terms the novel suggests it would itself use to judge others.

But we find that the novel turns against the Crawfords and not Mansfield. As the third volume opens, the crisis in Fanny's and Henry's relationship develops ("Fanny had by no means forgotten Mr. Crawford, when she awoke the next morning" [III, chap. 1, 312]). At this point the insight of the Crawfords is put, of course with a significantly different emphasis, by Sir Thomas, as he explains to Fanny that Henry wants to marry her. He finds her in her room, without a fire.

"I am aware that there has been sometimes, in some points, a
misplaced distinction; but I think too well of you, Fanny, to
suppose you will ever harbour resentment on that account.—
You have an understanding, which will prevent you from re-
ceiving things only in part, and judging partially by the
event.—You will take in the whole of the past, you will consider times, persons, and probabilities, and you will feel that
they were not least your friends who were educating and pre-
paring you for that mediocrity of condition which *seemed* to be
your lot. . . . I am sure you will not disappoint my opinion of
you, by failing at any time to treat your Aunt Norris with the
respect and attention that are due to her." [III, chap. 1, 313]

Painful as this speech is to read, it is not intended wholly to
damn Sir Thomas. The praise of Fanny's understanding
points up a way of arriving at sound judgments which the
novel approves. And even the fact that this sound method
leads to an apology for Mrs. Norris is not wholly disparaged:
Mrs. Norris, as Fanny's aunt, deserves respect, even if, as an
individual, she is reprehensible. This paradoxical morality
prevails in *Mansfield Park* at the same time that its essential
failures are amply demonstrated. The Sir Thomas who speaks
here is still a man who has not come to see what the life he has
arranged for himself at Mansfield and the people with whom
he has surrounded himself are really like. We know therefore
that Sir Thomas has not here come to a requisite self-
realization. Yet the crassness of judgment he displays in this
passage is never repudiated; the terms persevere; we become
unhappily conscious that the author shares them; and we remain so as we read on.

Having refused Henry, Fanny is banished to Portsmouth—to learn "the value of a good income," as Sir Thomas says (III, chap. 6, 369). It is a cold welcome she receives. "With an acknowledgement that he had quite forgot
her, Mr. Price now received his daughter" (III, chap. 7, 380).

But, as often with Fanny, the strictly personal slight pains her less than the question of principle—

> to have scarcely an enquiry made after Mansfield! It did pain her to have Mansfield forgotten; the friends who had done so much—the dear, dear friends! But here one subject swallowed up all the rest. . . . Yet she thought it would not have been so at Mansfield. No, in her uncle's house there would have been a consideration of times and seasons, a regulation of subject, a propriety, an attention towards every body which there was not here. [III, chap. 7, 382]

Many things crystallize in this passage. The passage confirms, in its repetition of Sir Thomas's own praise of Fanny's understanding, Fanny's crucial role: we see Fanny in her achieved place as the collective memory of Mansfield Park. It is not simply that, absent from Mansfield, Fanny remembers it so passionately. It is that we see here, in the echo of Sir Thomas's terms of judgment, and in the echo of the failure of the others at Mansfield, that Fanny holds the recollection of value in her own person. For Sir Thomas himself, in his apology to Fanny, has shown that attention toward everyone was *not* present at Mansfield; and that if there was consideration of times, seasons, and subject, this consideration actively inhered in Fanny alone. So in this passage and the others like it at Portsmouth Fanny assumes her final stature as the inheritor of Mansfield Park.

But just as this occurs, as a kind of confirming affirmation of the power of memory, at just this point the failure of Fanny's memory also crystallizes. She remembers Mansfield inaccurately. But the novel lets this lapse pass, indulges the extra emphasis ("the dear, dear friends!"), and assents to Fanny's rather more grand restatement of this same faulty picture when she later recalls "the elegance, propriety, regularity, harmony . . . the peace and tranquillity of Mansfield." "At Mansfield, no sounds of contention, no raised voice, no abrupt bursts, no tread of violence . . . every body had their due importance; every body's feelings were consulted" (III, chap. 8, 391–92). Here absence becomes an occasion for the buildup of Mansfield Park, and the crassness of Sir Thomas's speech to Fanny returns as an element of the novel's main theme. Where the novel had turned previously on the question of what was remembered, on the scrutiny of recollection, now actual relationships, "the whole of the past," become obscured by what I think we have to call simply class feeling. The distaste expressed in the novel for the poverty of Portsmouth allows the inflation of Mansfield, the convenient omission from memory of the whole of the past. Asked to celebrate the rise of Fanny to her full role as the collective memory of Mansfield, we are urged to forget that Mansfield itself may not be worth Fanny's words of praise. Once again the novel follows the procedure of the planters in their social acclimatization in the home country. Mansfield Park, insofar as it represents the mother country, comes to be seen as itself the source of value, as if it were Britain that was shipping wealth to the West Indies. Inaccurate as this view may be, it accurately represents Britain's developed attitude toward its colonies. In the novel Fanny comes from Portsmouth to Mansfield and enriches it, but the stressed relationship is Portsmouth's (and the Prices') dependence on Mansfield.

It is important to note that this manner of apology, in which in order to affirm tradition actuality must be blurred or forgotten, is characteristic of the conservative defense of landed capitalism. Especially one notes the correspondence between Austen's mystification of the source of value and the mystification, for example in Burke, of the relationship between labor and wealth.

> Good order is the foundation of all good things. To be enabled to acquire, the people, without being servile, must be tractable and obedient. The magistrate must have his reverence, the laws their authority. The body of the people must not find the principles of natural subordination by art rooted out of their minds. They must respect that property of which they cannot

partake. They must labour to obtain what by labour can be obtained; and when they find, as they commonly do, the success disproportioned to the endeavour, they must be taught their consolation in the final proportions of eternal justice.[28]

Jane Austen and Edmund Burke have much in common.[29] *Reflections on the Revolution in France* and *Mansfield Park* are key documents in the conservative history of the old regime, paeans to a flawed but apotheosized landed capitalism. They share a common philosophy: that morality is the source of social power and that religion is the basis of morality; that the family is the microcosm of the state and that human perfection can be found only by means of civil society. Their mutual aim is "at once to preserve and to reform."[30] But the intention to maintain the extant system involves in both writers an insistent mystification of the extant system and of its origins. Burke's commitment to the idea that good order is the foundation of all good things receives its fictional expression in *Mansfield park*. But, just as in Burke good order can only by a

28. Edmund Burke, *Reflections on the Revolution in France*, ed. with an introduction by Conor Cruise O'Brien (Harmondsworth: Penguin Books, 1969), p. 372.

29. A point many people have made. See, for instance, Alistair M. Duckworth, *The Improvement of the Estate: A Study of Jane Austen's Novels* (Baltimore: Johns Hopkins Press, 1971), pp. 45–48. Maurice J. Quinlan, *Victorian Prelude: A History of English Manners, 1700–1830* (repr. Hamden, Conn.: Anchon Books, 1965; first published New York: Columbia University Press, 1941), argues interestingly that "in England a conservative system of manners was to be fathered by the reaction to [the French Revolution]. Although it would require a few more decades for Victorianism to become general, the period 1790–1800 marked a turning point in English social history" (p. 69). Quinlan goes on to document the conscious conservative propaganda of manners by such people as Hannah More, Mrs. Trimmer, and the writers of books of manners. He quotes the following from Burke (p. 69): "Manners are of more importance than laws. Upon them in a great measure the laws depend. The law touches us but here and there and now and then. Manners are what vex or soothe, corrupt or purify, exalt or debase, barbarize or refine us, by a constant, steady, uniform, and insensible operation, like that of the air we breathe." Edmund Bertram—and one presumes his creator—would have heartily approved.

30. Burke, *Reflections*, p. 280.

convenient lapse of memory and observation be shown to be the foundation of all good things, so in Austen the peace and tranquillity of Mansfield can only by Fanny's misremembering be said to amount to that rather different quality: harmony.[31]

Having followed the conservative argument through, one returns to the essential contradiction of *Mansfield Park*, the estate's dependence on Antigua. The novel portrays, meticulously, the condition of the gentry whose life Jane Austen wishes to preserve and to reform. The historical crisis of the gentry and their international sources of wealth are integrally plotted. Nor does the novel allow any illusion that the gentry might find in themselves the qualities to save themselves. Fanny must save them. Yet Fanny is not her family's daughter—she is not, that is, as is Elizabeth Bennet in *Pride and Prejudice*, the representative of a vital middle class. Fanny is plucked from Portsmouth but so fully internalizes Mansfield's ideology that she turns against Portsmouth and comes to represent Mansfield itself. But consequently, as I have argued, the source of Fanny's own makeup remains mysterious. She is not educated to be the formidable woman she becomes but springs on the novel full grown. Though she suffers the failures of Mansfield, she displays the greatest concern for its

---

31. Cf. Alfred Cobban, *Edmund Burke and the Revolt against the Eighteenth Century: A Study of the Political and Social Thinking of Burke, Wordsworth, Coleridge, and Southey* (2d ed.; London: George Allen & Unwin, 1960). Cobban, essentially sympathetic to Burke, yet argues that in maintaining that human nature was defined by what had always been, Burke reduced his appeal to human nature to an "appeal to the past" (p. 79). Whereas Burke insisted on the facts, "the trouble was that the facts were changing" (p. 52). Consequently the difficulty with Burke's idea of liberty "was that, as things were, liberties were so arbitrary and unequally divided that they were equivalent to privileges, and so in practice tended to become merely a defence to the privileged classes. Nor, taking the permanence of the existing order for granted, did he look forward to any extension of privileges to the rest of the community" (p. 57). *Mansfield Park*, like Burke's *Reflections*, is a book ostensibly in defense of liberty which is actually only a defense of the privileged classes.

preservation: she alone of all the family questions Sir Thomas about his Antiguan experiences; though her own experience damns Mansfield, it is precisely her own experience that Fanny denies. Put out of mind is the history of the estate actually witnessed and approved is the history of the estate as an ideological possibility. Only in this way can the novel affirm that tremendously potent idea of the landed system that dominated so much English writing during the nineteenth century. In *Mansfield Park* the thrust of meaning asserts a system rooted in land and tradition, glossing over its actual basis in capital and empire. The novel demonstrates, in its particular use of memory, the kind of forgetfulness that an affirmation of landed capitalism necessitated in 1812–13.

II *Shirley*

i

The importance of the years 1812–13 to Charlotte Brontë is of course significantly different from their importance to Jane Austen. But to set *Shirley* next to *Mansfield Park* is first to appreciate the continuity of a special history, the history of women's feelings, and thus of repression and fulfillment, in the "middle ranks" of English society during the Industrial Revolution. Eugene Forçade said of *Shirley* that "as a picture of society, the novel could have been called *Shirley, or the condition of women in the English middle class.*"[32] This, then, is the substantive continuity. Both authors view human possibilities by reference to the condition of middle-class women; and this defining place, from which both authors begin and out of which both develop their responses, generates the problem each attempts to grasp and solve: How, under what circumstances of character and society, can fulfillment be achieved?

32. *Revue des deux mondes*, November 15, 1849; quoted in Miriam Allott, ed., *The Brontës: The Critical Heritage* (London and Boston: Routledge & Kegan Paul, 1974), p. 143.

We can separate within this problem two related but distinct questions: What qualities are necessary in the individual for her to realize a full life? And what social circumstances will nurture individual fulfillment? In different novels of Austen and Brontë these two questions, though both are always put, receive different emphases. What distinguishes *Mansfield Park* and *Shirley* is that the *relation* of the two questions is central. Put differently, both novels explore the compatibilities and incompatibilities between the special history of women's feelings and the broader English history, the total transformation of life in this era.

In focusing on this critical *relation* both authors face difficult issues of ideology and form. Both *Pride and Prejudice* and *Jane Eyre*, for all their differences, have available a structural principle organic to the content explored, the structure of courtship. Both novels trace the career of a single dominating character. This identification with one woman's fate at once yields expression to women's progressive aspirations and provides a social agency for fulfillment: a literally and symbolically liberating marriage. In these novels, where the emphasis falls on possibility rather than threat, the powerful historic forces of change which propel individuals and which individuals propel gain voice in a compatible narrative structure. The novels in this way show us the society but do not show us the novelist in the act of historical reflection.

But once Austen and Brontë try to narrate an individual career within a fully realized society, the organic development of form out of content becomes problematic. The structure of courtship, for example, no longer serves, for it allows expression mainly to an individual rather than a social point of view. The absence of courtship as an organizing principle throws both *Mansfield Park* and *Shirley* into a formal crisis. If it is clear that the structure of courtship will no longer do, it is not clear what will. Moreover, the formal crisis is part of a larger ideological crisis. For in *Mansfield Park* and *Shirley*, Jane Austen and Charlotte Brontë find the Tory gentry society they want to preserve and to reform threatened by the very social forces with which, in *Pride and Prejudice* and *Jane Eyre*, they had themselves earlier identified.

In *Mansfield Park* women's aspiration for fulfillment is effectively submerged in a conservative defense of landed capitalism. The novel establishes the estate as the locus of value and subsumes everything to that primary center. It creates, as well, a complex structure of memory to validate a particular tradition. Although the novel argues that without this tradition civilized human relationships are unthinkable, the enacted values are disheartening. In the place of Elizabeth Bennet's energy we have Fanny's acquiescent, obsequious humility; instead of a vitalizing merger of trade and land, skeptical wit and lord-of-the manor stolidity, we have a staunchly paternalistic, religiously somber structure of feeling; instead of the active creation of the self we have Fanny's "given," technically unjustified character. In *Mansfield Park*, in short, the effort to preserve and to reform amounts mainly to retrenchment.

But if *Mansfield Park* is in this way about history, it is not a historical novel in the sense that it narrates actual historical incidents. The novel records and interprets a particular tradition of behavior: what is at issue is not in any way a question of *fact*. For Austen the continuity of present and past is kept integral and is enforced in memory; but what is remembered is something more subtle, less tangible, and more powerful than past events: it is the idea of the past. In *Shirley*, however, the special history of women's feelings is placed in relation to particular events that actually occurred in a particular place, for particular reasons, in a particular way. Written in 1848–49 about the years 1811–12, the novel poses explicit historical problems. Consequently, a persistent dispute in criticism of the novel has been whether Charlotte Brontë wrote an accurate account of the historical events, whether she did full justice to the "facts." The novel promises "something real, cool, solid"[33] and underlines the novelist's role as historian. We are urged to make connections between the political, religious, and sexual themes of the novel, to see the action as a single unit of regional and national history. But Brontë's insistence on a particular history forces us back, inevitably, on the questions: What *was* the actual history? Do we find it in the novel?

ii

In the winter of 1811–12, framework knitters in and around Nottingham began organized attacks on various manufacturing premises for the purpose of destroying what, ironically, we have come to call "labor-saving machinery." (The incendiary "Luddism" derives from the name of General Ludd or Ned Ludd, the mythic figure under whose direction the workers ostensibly acted and in whose name warnings were issued to manufacturers and magistrates.) From Nottingham Luddism soon spread to south Lancashire and to the West Riding of Yorkshire. A Luddite gathering was reported at Leeds in January 1812, and regular reports of Luddite activity continued from that date until the late summer. On March 24 textile mills at Rawdon, eight miles from Leeds, were attacked and machinery destroyed. In the West Riding the machines destroyed were mechanical shears or shearing frames intended to replace the large, hand-operated shearing scissors used by the croppers to finish the cloth. These hand shears were a full four feet long and weighed about forty pounds. Because skillful use of the shears significantly affected the value of the cloth, the croppers were aristocrats of their trade, in a good position to keep control over their work, and protected by the old paternalistic legislation against gig mills. They saw the introduction of mechanical shears into the big shops as a threat not only to their preeminent position but to their very liveli-

33. *Shirley: A Tale* (2 vols.; Oxford and Boston: At the Shakespeare Head Press, Basil Blackwell and Houghton Mifflin, 1931), I, chap. 1, 1. Further references are found in the text.

hoods. Their complaints, aggravated by the generally poor state of the trade as a consequence of the Orders in Council, could not be translated into trade-union activity because of the severe restrictions of the Combination Acts.

In April the attack at Rawdon was followed by a dramatic assault on Joseph Foster's factory at Horbury, near Wakefield. Three hundred men, reportedly led and followed by a mounted party with drawn swords, sacked and burned Foster's mill on April 9. Two days later came the attack of which Charlotte Brontë writes, on the mill of William Cartwright at Rawfolds, in the Spen Valley. But Cartwright had determined to resist: barricaded inside his mill with four of his workmen and five soldiers, he met an estimated 150 Luddites with determined musket fire. After a battle of about thirty minutes, during which two of the Luddites were fatally wounded and an indeterminate number hurt, the men retreated, repulsed successfully for the first time in the West Riding. Two weeks later, on April 27, the manufacturer William Horsfall of Ottiwells, near Huddersfield, chairman of the Huddersfield Committee for the Suppression of the Outrages, was assassinated while out riding alone. In May eleven pairs of shears belonging to Cartwright and sent to Wakefield to be sharpened were destroyed. The Orders in Council were repealed in June, and although Luddite incidents continued into the summer—and in the Midlands until 1816-17—they petered out in Yorkshire by the fall of 1812.[34]

34. For Luddism, Chartism, and their relation to *Shirley*, I consulted Asa Briggs, "Private and Social Themes in *Shirley*," *Brontë Society Transactions*, 13, no. 3 (1958); Lord Byron, "Maiden Speech in the House of Lords, 27 February 1812," in *Works of Lord Byron: Letters and Journals*, ed. Rowland E. Prothero (New York: Octagon Books, 1966 [first published London: John Murray, 1898-1901]), II, 425-30; F. O. Darvall, *Popular Disturbances and Public Order in Regency England*, with a new introduction by Angus MacIntyre (London: Oxford University Press, 1969 [1934]); Elizabeth Cleghorn Gaskell, *Life of Charlotte Brontë* (London: J. M. Dent, 1958); J. L. and Barbara Hammond, *The Skilled Laborer* (London: Longman's, Green, 1919) and *The Age of the Chartists* (London: Longman's, Green, 1930); E. J. Hobsbawm, "The Machine Breakers," in his *Labouring Men: Studies in the*

Yorkshire Luddism ended formally in the trial of the Luddites held at York Castle between January 2 and 12, 1813. Sixty-four men were charged with a variety of offenses; the twenty-nine who were finally convicted fall into three groups: one group, associated with the Halifax Republican John Baines, was charged with administering an illegal Luddite oath to John McDonald (an informer; all authorities agree these men were framed); the main group was charged with "beginning to demolish William Cartwright's mill" or similar offenses (breaking shearing frames, stealing arms) or, in the cases of George Mellor (leader of the West Riding Luddites), Thomas Smith, and William Thorpe, with the murder of Horsfall; and a final group was charged with burglaries of various kinds, associated in the official mind with Luddism but not in any obvious way connected with it.

The Brontës were as a family passionately engaged with politics; few events in history so fired Charlotte Brontë's im-

---

History of Labour (New York: Basic Books, 1964); Ivy Holgate, "The Structure of *Shirley*," *Brontë Society Transactions*, 14, no. 2 (1963); Patricia Hollis, *The Pauper Press: A Study in Working-Class Radicalism of the 1830s* (London: Oxford University Press, 1970); John James, *The History of Bradford and Its Parish, with Additions and Continuations to the Present Time* (London: Longmans, Green, Reader, & Dyer, 1841, and Bradford: Henry Gaskarth, 1866); the Leeds *Mercury* and the Leeds *Intelligencer* for 1811–14; Richard Offor, "The Brontës—Their Relation to the History and Politics of Their Time," *Brontë Society Transactions*, 10, no. 4 (1943); A. J. Peacock, *Bradford Chartism, 1838–1840*, Borthwick Papers no. 36 (York: University of York, 1969); Frank Peel, *Spen Valley: Past and Present* (Heckmondwike: T. W. Senior, 1893) and *The Risings of the Luddites* (Heckmondwike: T. W. Senior, 1880); *Report of the Proceedings under Commission of Oyer and Terminer and Gaol Delivery, for the County of York, Held at the Castle of York, before Sir Alexander Thomson, Knight, One of the Barons of the Exchequer; and Sir Simon Le Blanc, Knight, One of the Justices of the Court of King's Bench, from the 2nd to the 12th of January 1813* (London: Luke Hansard, [1813]); George Rudé, *The Crowd in History: A Study of Popular Disturbances in France and England, 1730–1848* (New York: John Wiley, 1964); Malcolm I. Thomis, *The Luddites: Machine Breaking in Regency England* (New York: Schocken Books, 1972); Thompson, *Making of the English Working Class*; and Herbert E. Wroot, "The Persons and Places of the Brontë Novels," *Brontë Society Transactions*, 3, no. 4 (1939).

agination as Wellington's protracted struggle against Napoleon. She was familiar with the history of the years 1811–13,
then, from her reading as a girl, and had early established deep
emotional commitments to the Tory view of English history
during the years of war. But the Brontë household received
both the Tory Leeds *Intelligencer* and "the organ of the half-
Whig, half-Radical, middle class,"[35] the Leeds *Mercury*. Interestingly, when Charlotte Brontë set out to write *Shirley*, she
sent for the old files not of the *Intelligencer* but of the Leeds
Mercury, a point I will discuss below. For the moment I want
to try to recreate some of the tone and substance of the Luddite years by reference to these two papers.

In late 1811 and early 1812, when Luddism erupts, both
papers are full of alarming reports about the general collapse of
law and order. The record is of widespread unrest, a turbulence so general that not only does the distinction between
industrial and political—upon which so much academic debate has focused—seem abstruse, but so does the distinction
between political and criminal. "Nightly depredations" are
regularly noted; on January 18 the *Mercury* reports in one
breath the news of frame breaking at Nottingham and the
establishment of an "association of police" at Skipton and
Wakefield; and it attributes, in a lump, to frame breaking,
robbery, and "banditry" the breakdown of civil order; these
are the reasons why "neither persons nor property can be
considered safe either by day or night." Both papers follow
closely, and report religiously, the spread of associations of
police from community to community. Burglaries, arms stealing, machine breaking, food riots, the murder of Horsfall and
of Spencer Perceval, the prime minister, are taken together as
signs of a discontent dangerously near insurrection.

The *Intelligencer* and the *Mercury* are broadly at odds in
their analysis of events. Indeed, the *Intelligencer* writes ven-
omously that the blame for unrest and disaffection should be

35. Thompson, *Making of the English Working Class*, p. 613.

put on the Leeds *Mercury* itself, "which by its weekly Prospec-
tus, is making the most dreadful inroads into the peace, tran-
quility, and loyalty of this populous district" (January 18,
1812). The "labouring poor" would not be discontented were
it not for the agitation caused by the editorials of the *Mercury*.

> Are the times awful and alarming? no hint is given of nations
> being punished for their wickedness—no christian [sic] call is
> made to the exercise of patience and *self-reformation:* but all
> eyes are perpetually directed to the Helm of State... as the
> *only* cause of every public and private calamity.
>   Are a lawless rabble in a neighboring county destroying the
> property of their employers.... They are directed to seek re-
> dress from Government itself; and in what way a mob will seek
> redress, has been fatally tried in France! [January 18, 1812]

Against this somewhat hysterical editorial rhetoric the *Mercury*, at its most lucid, opposes matter-of-factness, insisting on
the Orders in Council as the cause of distress and characterizing
the destruction of machinery as mindless, impolitic, and
dangerous but perhaps explicable. The two principal causes of
Luddism are "the price of the necessaries of life, and the use of
machinery calculated to diminish manual labour in that particular branch of the trade to which it is applied" (April 18,
1812). If "the state of the country is, indeed, awfully alarming," the explosion that may come will be the result of "that
unhappy system which has been so long persevered in by the
Ministers of this Country" (May 16, 1812). The *Mercury* is
also much more clear, or rather much more precise, about
what is at stake: "It must be obvious to all," says a leader on
April 18, 1812, "that private property must be held sacred,
and that no tyranny is so intolerable as the tyranny of the
mob." Of course the *Mercury* too, as the voice of the manufacturers, is vociferous in its resistance to the "tyranny of the
mob"—the phrase coming readily, quickly, by instinct to the
pen of the editorial writer. The *Mercury* nevertheless is rarely
so rabid as the *Intelligencer* or so wholly unable to understand
the situation of the working people as to approach the follow-

ing, from the *Intelligencer* of March 30, 1812: "On the subject
of EMPLOYMENT, many respectable individuals, as well as
workmen in general, for want of a little reflection, seem to
have fallen into error. *However clamourously men may demand
work, no set of men in society can by law, justice, or reason, be called
upon to provide work for any other set of men.*"

This sort of Malthusian vindictiveness does not appear in
the *Mercury* because the *Mercury* sees Luddism, indeed struggles hard to control the interpretation of Luddism, as caused
by industrial conditions that a change in government policy
would quickly improve. The *Mercury* argues, indeed, that machinery itself is not the true issue but the symbolic object on
which the frustrated workmen have fastened to protest the
depression in trade. Critical of the ministers, the *Mercury* is
eager to dissociate its criticism from disloyalty or insurrectionary activity, and thus argues in edition after edition that
Luddism is a cry for help rather than a political movement
with political implications, dangerous implications that might
be attributed to the *Mercury* itself and those for whom it
speaks. Therefore the analysis of Luddism as revolutionary
upsurge comes from the ever self-righteous *Intelligencer:*

> He must be ignorant in the extreme who does not see that the
> ravages of a lawless mob, assembled at midnight, in silence,
> disguised, armed, organised, without the fear of God before
> their eyes, and inspired with high sentiments of their own
> prowess, are not likely to be confined to the proprietors of
> *frames* and *mills.* Who does not see that such outrages affect the
> very vitals of society. . .?
> The question of machinery involves every form of contriv-
> ance from the dressing-shears to those shears with which the
> wool is separated from the sheep:—from the *plough* to the
> *kneading-trough.* . . . And every attempt to mislead the minds of
> the unskilful multitude to attribute the unavoidable hardships
> they suffer, either directly from the visitations of divine provi-
> dence, or mediately from the common enemy of their country
> and of mankind, to a wrong cause, is deserving of severe rep-
> rehensions, as cruel to the poor, as an enemy to soci-
> ety.   [April 20, 1812]

If these excerpts demonstrate something of the texture of life and argument, of the tone of ideological dispute, among the "educated classes" during the years of Luddism; and if they show that, in the mind of ruling groups, the distinction between "industrial" and "political" and between "political" and "insurrectionary" was a very fine one indeed, usually one to which little attention was paid in feeling, nonetheless the exchanges between the two newspapers leave unstated the full nature of the issues. What remains submerged is suggested in a resolution passed on February 17, 1812, at a general meeting of the merchants and manufacturers of Leeds. These gentlemen declare:

> We cannot sufficiently reprobate the Attempts now making, in Defiance of the Laws, by the labouring Classes, in various Parts of the Country, by their unlawful Clubs, Committees, Weekly Subscriptions, by Threats and Personal Injury, by Violence and Destruction of Property, to fix the Prices of Labour, to direct in this Free State how Capital shall be employed... and especially to prevent Use of Machinery, cherished and encouraged by the Laws and the Government, as absolutely necessary to maintain the British Manufacture in that Pre-eminence they have acquired. [Leeds *Intelligencer*, May 23, 1812]

I don't know if one could present this passage, in the history of Luddism, as a "bare" fact; but it certainly speaks, in a very direct, indeed a very bare, language, to what was seen to be at issue. And it allows us to begin to approach Charlotte Brontë's understanding of the history as it appears in *Shirley*. Machinery is named here as a subject of contention, but the essential issue is one of control, of how, "in this Free State," as the manufacturers so bluntly put it, "Capital shall be employed." The manufacturers are thus blunt because their relationship with their workers is not one of general or broadly social intercourse but the direct relationship of the workplace. They assert their rights in the unqualified terms of laissez faire—which is to say that the freedom they see to be at issue is *their* freedom to do as they like with *their* property. If it is clear that the assertion of such freedom sparked committees, subscriptions, violence, and the destruction of property, I find it difficult to say, judging from the sources I have read, whether the full implications of their position can be said to have dawned on the manufacturers as a body. The assertion of their freedom abolished, in theory and in fact, the freedom of workers to control their work, and violated the system of work relationships around which life in the woolen districts—and elsewhere—had been organized for generations. If the workmen's campaign to retain control over their labor appears simply unlawful and irrational, as the manufacturers' resolution suggests, then the fact that one freedom is definitively opposed to another becomes hard to see. The *Mercury* often suggests, in terms that become increasingly common, that the worker and the manufacturer ought to be "the best of friends" (February 29, 1812). But insofar as we grant this expression some genuine feeling, it is made at best from a great distance, a distance enforced by habit, experience, and centrally perhaps self-interest. The point is that from this distance the worker's life remains unseen and opaque. During the years of Luddism, moreover, war, domestic insurrection, the struggle between Tory and Whig all increase the already great distance between the classes, and consequently obscure the issues that created the Luddite risings. The unrestricted introduction of certain kinds of machinery, the rush into the system of gig mills, meant to the workers that they were to be divested, more or less at a stroke, of the way of life that they considered not simply traditional but *just* and *right*, a way of life the center of which was a system of control by the workers over their work.[36]

36. Cf. ibid., pp. 600–601, and Harry Braverman's analysis of the development of labor processes in his *Labor and Monopoly Capital: The Degradation of Work in the Twentieth Century* (New York and London: Monthly Review Press, 1974). "The control of humans over the labor process," Braverman argues (p. 193), is increased by machinery, but in practice this increase can be concretely understood only

I have lingered on this point, familiar perhaps as it is, because it seems to me the crucial one to make about the political confusion and the apparent disunity of *Shirley*. For *Shirley*, like so many of the novels about class conflict published in the 1840s, treats the issue of class without reference to work relationships. The mill owner Robert Moore confronts his workers, verbally and physically, at a number of points in the novel. But we never see the actual process of work, the relationships of work, and therefore we never experience the full meaning of the conflict over machinery. The absence of working as a *realized* activity in the novel exposes the central limitation of the ideology Charlotte Brontë expresses; it is the main thing she does not see. Consequently she poses one of the novel's key problems incorrectly, misperceives what's truly at issue, and cannot therefore engage the problem fruitfully. And this failure is especially troublesome because she sees the problem of *women's* lives with great clarity, and wants to assert that at the heart of the society's malaise lies a single problem, common to a number of oppressed groups, but chiefly women

---

in the social setting in which machinery is being developed. And this social setting is, and has been from the beginnings of the development of machinery in its modern forms, one in which humanity is sharply divided, and nowhere more sharply divided than in the labor process itself. The mass of humanity is subjected to the labor process for the purposes of those who control it rather than for any general purposes of "humanity" as such. In thus acquiring concrete form, the control of humans over the labor process turns into its opposite and becomes the control of the labor process over the mass of humans. Machinery comes into the world not as the servant of "humanity" but as the instrument of those to whom the accumulation of capital gives the *ownership* of the machines. The capacity of humans to control the labor process through machinery is seized upon by management from the beginning of capitalism as the *prime means whereby production may be controlled not by the direct producer but by the owners and representatives of capital.* Thus, in addition to its technical function of increasing the productivity of labor—which would be the mark of machinery under any social system—machinery also has in the capitalist system the function of divesting the mass of workers of their control over their own labor. [Braverman's italics.]

and workers. Here, for example, Caroline Helstone considers the life of "old maids":

> People hate to be reminded of ills they are unable or unwilling to remedy: such reminder, in forcing on them a sense of their own incapacity, or a more painful sense of an obligation to make some unpleasant effort, troubles their ease and shakes their self-complacency. Old maids, like the houseless and the unemployed poor, should not ask for a place and an occupation in the world: the demand disturbs the happy and rich. [II, chap. 22, 82]

"Old maids, like the houseless and the unemployed poor"— the apposition, casual as it appears, for that very reason underlines the argument being made about the essential unity of interest and of position. Perhaps, within the terms of this passage, the suggestion of identity holds, especially since the image of relationships expressed is deeply paternalistic—the rich have an "obligation" to the poor. But whereas the novel dramatizes with great effect the lives of old maids, and of women in their relation to men and society, it treats the workers differently. Consider the confrontation between Moore and the delegation of his workmen led by Moses Barraclough[37] and Noah o' Tim's in the chapter Brontë gracelessly titles "Noah and Moses." The Luddite leaders are satirized as drunken, Methodist opportunists and contrasted with the good worker William Farren. Although Noah urges Moore to

37. Charlotte Brontë may have found the name and to some extent the character of Barraclough in the Leeds *Mercury*, which printed the following on July 11, 1812:

> A person of the name of Barrowclough, of Holmfirth, a Corporal in the Upper Agbrig Local Militia, has been apprehended and charged on his own confession, with having been concerned in the murder of Mr Horsfall, and with having assisted in the attack on the Shearing Mill of Mr Cartwright, at Rawfolds; but it appears, on investigation, that Barrowclough was at York with the regiment at the time the murder took place. This singular information of accusing himself of crimes of which he is not, and could not be guilty, is attributed to a mental infirmity under which he is said to labour when he has 'put an enemy in his mouth to steal away his brains.'

leave the country, Barraclough more practically asks that
Moore part with his " 'infernal machinery, and tak' on more
hands.' " Moore responds with a military flourish (" 'Silence!
You have had your say and now I will have mine.' ") and the
common sense of laissez faire:

> "You request me to part with my machinery; in case I refuse,
> you threaten me. I *do* refuse. . . . Here I stay; and by this mill I
> stand; and into it I will convey the best machinery inventors
> can furnish. . . . Suppose that building [his mill] was a ruin and
> I was a corpse, what then?—you lads behind these two
> scamps, would that stop invention or exhaust sci-
> ence? . . . Another and better gig-mill would rise on the ruins
> of this. . . . Hear me!—I'll make cloth as I please. . . . In its
> manufacture I will employ what means I choose. Whosoever,
> after hearing this, shall dare interfere with me, may just take
> the consequences." [I, chap. 8, 149–50]

Moore then calls out the constable Sugden, who has been
hiding in readiness in Moore's mill, and has Moses arrested for
the destruction of some of his frames. Pacing pistol in hand
before his factory after this flamboyant encounter, Moore is
approached by William Farren—modestly, as Brontë carefully
points out.

> "Ye see we're ill off,—vary ill off: wer families is poor and
> pined. We're thrown out o' work wi' these frames: we can get
> nought to do: we can earn nought. . . . I'm not for shedding
> blood . . . and I'm not for pulling down mills and breaking
> machines . . . but I'll talk,—I'll mak as big a din as ever I can.
> Invention may be all right, but I know it isn't right for poor
> folks to starve. Them that governs mun find a way to help
> us. . . ." [I, chap. 8, 150–51]

But even here Moore is hard, with a hardness Brontë makes us
understand she doesn't approve: " 'Talk to me no more about
machinery; I will have my own way. I shall get new frames in
to-morrow: If you broke these, I would still get more. *I'll never
give in*' " (I, chap. 8, 151; Brontë's italics).

Although Moore takes steps to provide Farren with some
work—careful, however, to keep his benevolence hidden from

Farren and the other workers—the novel shows him to be wrongly unbending in the face of want. No doubt he is, but that is beside the point. Moore puts the manufacturers' case in the standard terms: Brontë intends him to appear arrogant, but it's clear he is no more arrogant than the manufacturers and merchants of Leeds who assembled in February 1812 to take measures against the Luddites. "I'll make cloth as I please" may not be patrician but it states with complete accuracy the tone and the tenor of laissez faire practice. In contrast, Farren complains about hunger in a way that is wholly inaccurate. He speaks as if being in work and being out of work were the essential question, whereas the essential question is: Who will control the work? Charlotte Brontë allows Farren to speak of himself as "poor." He may be poor from her point of view, but as a cropper he would not have spoken of himself in that way, for he would have been a man at the very pinnacle of working-class society in the woolen districts. For Farren the issue could not have been simply the loss of work, but the loss of a way of life, of a trade for which he had worked a long apprenticeship, of a preeminence among his fellows, of a whole network of values and judgments about what is just and proper in human relationships. Farren speaks like a man who has no sense of his own rights in the realm of manufacture, whereas it was precisely the conflict over rights that caused Luddism. Beginning, then, with a formulation of conflict which is historically inaccurate and which projects an inaccurate picture of the society in which Farren and Moore live, Charlotte Brontë naturally has difficulty in bringing this false conflict to a true conclusion. But I am anticipating. Before moving to an examination of the unity of the novel, I want to return to the question of its use of history. Charlotte Brontë could write of women on the basis of her own experience; to write of Luddism and the conflict between workers and owners, she had to some extent to refer to historical sources.

Some critics of *Shirley* have been fortified by Brontë's recourse to the files of the Leeds *Mercury*. Andrew and Judith

Hook, for example, in an otherwise valuable introduction to the Penguin English Library edition, put the received opinion: "In sending for the files of the Leeds *Mercury* for the years 1812–1814 Charlotte Brontë showed her determination to respect the historical facts" (p. 19). It is puzzling that this judgment has become a commonplace of Brontë criticism, for it is certainly too quick and easy. In the first place it assumes that Luddism can properly be dealt with within the frame of 1812–14—an assumption I think is demonstrably unfounded. Second, it assumes that the Leeds *Mercury* contains "the historical facts"—an assumption that a brief glance at the Leeds *Mercury* will show to be very far from the truth. The *Mercury* was, it is important to remember, simply a newspaper, a record of the obvious (or some of the obvious) at the moment of its occurrence. A comparison of the Leeds *Mercury* and its Tory competitor, the *Intelligencer*, as I have already suggested, shows that even the obvious can appear quite differently to different observers. "The historical facts" appear in both papers as partly ideology, partly selective reportage, and partly hearsay. Even if one limits oneself to the "bare" facts, to what can indisputably be said to have happened, the Leeds *Mercury* is of only marginal use. Certainly it records machine breaking, arms stealing, and burglary. But its account of the attack on William Cartwright's mill contains few of the characterizing details that give this event body in the novel.

Asa Briggs judges Charlotte Brontë's reading of the Leeds *Mercury* in a more helpful way than do the Hooks: "There is a difference," he writes, "between Charlotte's consulting the old files of the Leeds *Mercury* and George Eliot's consulting the old files of *The Times* when she wrote *Felix Holt* and *Middlemarch*. Charlotte knew more or less what she would find."[38] But even here one wonders exactly what Briggs believes Charlotte Brontë knew—did she know "the facts"?— and one wants to distinguish between knowledge of the facts

38. Briggs, "Private and Social Themes in *Shirley*," p. 205.

and the kind of knowledge a novelist might need to write a work of fiction. My own sense is that the Leeds *Mercury* can have been of little use in establishing the kind of dramatic record of history a novelist might be able to use; if Charlotte Brontë had had to depend merely on the Leeds *Mercury* to write *Shirley*, she would have faced a very hard task indeed. On the other hand, the choice of the *Mercury* over the *Intelligencer* suggests to me that she consulted it to learn what she might *not* in fact have known, or what she might have known only, as it were, from the other side—the case of the manufacturers. I believe Brontë read the *Mercury* to gain a fuller insight into Robert Moore, a fuller insight into the views of those men in Yorkshire whose attitude toward Wellington and his war was not her own. As my excerpts above show, in this respect the *Mercury* can be said to contain "the historical facts."

If Brontë read the *Mercury* for what she did *not* know, what were the sources of her knowledge, the sources that allow Asa Briggs to say she "knew more or less what she would find"? These sources—far richer than the newspaper files—were the firsthand accounts of Luddism she had from her father, and with which she grew up; the stories told her by Miss Wooler, whose school at Roe Head was located in what had been the setting of much Luddite activity years before; and the reminiscences of the men and women of the middle and working classes among whom she passed her time when visiting or out-of-doors. The oral history of Luddism was part of the atmosphere of the communities in which Charlotte Brontë came of age. But although we know this to be so, it is harder to say exactly what this oral tradition actually contained. Two sources are helpful in this respect: Frank Peel's *Risings of the Luddites*, already alluded to, and Elizabeth Gaskell's comments in her *Life of Charlotte Brontë*. From the former we can learn of the popular tradition, from the latter of the middle-class tradition to which Charlotte Brontë had more direct access.

The chief political event in *Shirley* is the attack on Moore's factory, an attack that, E. P. Thompson says, became "legendary" in the real history of the West Riding. Thompson also says that Brontë presents faithfully in *Shirley* the middle-class legend.[39] But certainly part of the record—in Peel, Gaskell, and *Shirley*—is the same, and contains information the newspapers did not carry. All three accounts stress the fearful aspect of the Luddites, especially the ominous *sound* of the men as they moved through the countryside in darkness. Here, in Peel's version, the Luddites march at night toward Cartwright's mill:

> As the heavy tread of the men falls on the hard road, many of the sleepers in the houses are awakened, and rushing to their windows peep stealthily forth and see the black compact masses, with the barrels of their guns and the dreadful looking hatchets and hammers gleaming dimly in the starlight, and then creep back to lay their heads on sleepless pillows, their teeth chattering with fear. They have heard many frightful tales of the doings of the dreaded Luddites.[40]

This melodramatic rendering is given almost identically in *Shirley* (II, chap. 19, 20–21) and in Gaskell's *Life*.[41] Peel's account of the attack on Cartwright's mill, told from the point of view of the men inside, is also substantially the same as Brontë's. Peel writes: "They can hear the trampling of many feet, a confused hum of voices, and then with a sudden and tremendous crash hundreds of great stones come bounding through the long lines of windows. . . . Then follows a terrific yell from the desperate multitude—a yell loud enough and wild enough to strike terror into the boldest heart."[42] In *Shirley*, Charlotte Brontë writes of the same event:

> A simultaneously-hurled volley of stones had saluted the broad front of the mill, with all its windows; and now every pane of every lattice lay in shattered and pounded fragments. A yell

39. Thompson, *Making of the English Working Class*, pp. 612–13.
40. Peel, *Risings of the Luddites*, p. 41.
41. Gaskell, *Life of Charlotte Brontë*, p. 71.
42. Peel, *Risings of the Luddites*, p. 45.

followed this demonstration—a rioters' yell—a North-of-
England—a Yorkshire—a West Riding—a West-Riding-
clothing-district-of-Yorkshire rioters' yell. You never heard
that sound, perhaps, reader? So much the better for your
ears—perhaps for your heart; since, if it rends the air in hate to
yourself, or to the men or principles you approve, the interests
which you wish well, Wrath wakens to the cry of Hate: the
Lion shakes his mane, and rises to the howl of the Hyena:
Caste stands up, ireful, against Caste; and the indignant,
wronged spirit of the Middle Rank bears down in zeal and
scorn on the famished and furious mass of the Operative Class.
It is difficult to be tolerant—difficult to be just—in such
moments. [II, chap. 19, 28]

Terry Eagleton, in his study of *Shirley*, complains that this
passage renders the structurally central attack on Moore's mill
"curiously empty—empty because the major protagonist, the
working class, is distinguished primarily by its absence." The
battle, he writes, is mainly allegorized or heard but not *seen;*
thus, in this the central clash between worker and owner, the
working class is "wholly invisible."[43] This judgment seems to
me perhaps more applicable to the novel as a whole than to the
portrayal of the scenes of attack. The novel is told from the
point of view of Robert Moore, Caroline Helstone, and Shirley Keeldar. We see through them, on the whole. Consequently the organization of the attack never makes real the
feelings, ideas, or experiences of the workers. But it is
nonetheless clear that the mark that the attack left on the
imagination of the district, of working class, gentry, and manufacturers, was in fact "curiously" centered on the terror that
the Luddites sparked in the ruling classes, a terror symbolized
by the Yorkshire yell and the sound of men marching. The
concentration of fear into a single image of a yell and into the
sound of attack does not seem to me to make the working-class
presence here less tangible—it did not seem so to Frank Peel,
who reports the popular tradition—but to record the profound

43. Terry Eagleton, *Myths of Power: A Marxist Study of the Brontës* (London: Macmillan, 1975), pp. 47–48.

disruption of social relationships in the years of the Luddite crisis. It is precisely the sense of something disembodied, of a force in the darkness, which adequately conveys the rupture of social convention, the break enacted in the extremity of armed conflict. Charlotte Brontë writes of the attack, in this respect, on the basis of a shared tradition. The absence of verisimilitude does not weaken the felt drama of events.

On the other hand, she writes of everything surrounding the attack with a careful selectivity. Both Peel and Gaskell report that Cartwright had fortified his mill indoors with huge spiked rollers on the stairs (he wounded himself on one of them after the attack) and a tub of vitriol at the top for use should the Luddites have succeeded in gaining entry.[44] These details, which would obviously have marred Robert Moore's image as hero, are suppressed. One of the soldiers in Cartwright's mill refused to fire because, he is quoted as saying, "I might hit some of my brothers."[45] We never hear of him. In the popular tradition Cartwright is said to have refused aid to the wounded before they identified the leaders of the attack, and the Luddites John Booth and Samuel Hartley, both of whom died shortly after the attack, were said to have been tortured.[46] Popular tradition aside, it is a fact that the men were moved to the Star Inn at Robert-town rather than to any closer quarters because the military were concerned about a popular show of sympathy and the gathering of a hostile crowd; that Hartley was buried at Halifax in a display of numbers; and that, fearful of unrest, the authorities stole Booth's body from the Star Inn for burial in Huddersfield before dawn to avoid the large crowds that were gathering.[47] After the attack, the community—working class and middle class alike—closed protectively around the wounded and the

44. Peel, *Risings of the Luddites*, p. 42; Gaskell, *Life of Charlotte Brontë*, pp. 70–71.
45. Peel, *Risings of the Luddites*, p. 46.
46. Ibid., pp. 52–53.
47. Ibid., pp. 53–54, and Leeds *Mercury*, April 18, 1812.

men in hiding; for months not a single Luddite connected with the raid could be traced for arrest.

In the novel these facts are unmentioned, the reaction to the raid is presented in very different terms, and the main middle-class protagonists—Cartwright and the Reverend Hammond Roberson, the latter fervent in his pursuit of the Luddites—come out of the clash as heroes. Charlotte Brontë goes so far as to write that the Luddite leaders "were not members of the operative class: they were chiefly 'downdraughts,' bankrupts, men always in debt and often in drink—men who had nothing to lose and much—in the way of character, and cleanliness—to gain" (II, chap. 22, 73). She didn't arrive at this conclusion by reading the Leeds *Mercury*, and these are not "the historical facts." Quite simply, at key points Brontë refuses to admit into the novel what actually happened; partly, as in the passage above, she resorts to what she must have known to be outright distortion; partly, as in her discussion of machinery, she is incapable of imagining the actual life of the workers. In this sense, *Shirley* uses history overtly to make an ideological judgment and prescription. It is important, especially in the face of the received opinion to the contrary, to say that Luddism is portrayed in the novel largely through the biased perspective of the ruling class. This bias pertains not simply to "facts" but to the emotional weight of the facts—Brontë is capable of the most predictable prejudice, as in her attack on the cleanliness of the Luddites. But having said this, I think it is also important to add that the full ideological statement of the novel comes out of the whole fiction, out of the whole of the dramatized action of the book. Brontë's class bias must be clearly seen; one cannot read the novel well if one ignores it; but neither are the politics of the novel and its political aim summed up or contained in Brontë's predictable class judgments. For Brontë tries in *Shirley* to merge into a single account the usual history portrayed in the English novel—the history of women's feelings, with its radical emphasis on the values of personal fulfillment—and the total history of the society. Now, in the late 1840s, the society Brontë depicts is an emerging industrial capitalism, specifically the society of the rural West Riding, where the woolen industry flourished. The special history of women, then, is set in relation to the history of the working class, of the landed gentry, the laissez faire industrialists, and the middle ranks. The ideological ambition of the novel is to discover and affirm in these interconnected histories a single source of value. The flawed rendering of Luddism damages the novel, but it is not on the basis of Luddism alone that one can either fully understand or judge *Shirley*.

iii

Criticism of *Shirley* has inevitably centered on the question of its unity: Brontë's aim to draw a picture of the whole has usually been seen as an impossible attempt to integrate too many unconnected themes, and to lead to such irrelevancies as the comic histories of the curates.[48] My own sense, however, is that the novel is remarkably unified. In the introductory chapters, in which the curates figure prominently and in which the various themes of the novel are swiftly introduced, a remarkably easy coherence is maintained. In these introductory scenes the theoretical difficulty of integrating a number of thematic elements is deftly overcome; what we notice, rather than disunity, are the possibilities of a subtle and complex plan for the novel.

The curates—Joseph Donne, Peter Malone, and David Sweeting—receive in the first chapter a deceptive slapstick treatment: Brontë indulges them but also lays bare their many failings. In the first place, the curates are utterly without piety. Brontë intends this failing to have a specific religious meaning—and thus the charge could not be more serious—but also to imply a broader moral failure. The curates' lack of

48. See Jacob Korg, "The Problem of Unity in *Shirley*," *Nineteenth Century Fiction*, 12 (September 1957), 125-36.

piety is the key flaw of a whole structure of values. We can see
what impiety means to Brontë in the following exchange between Malone and Donne's landlady, Mrs. John Gale, at
whose house the curates have gathered for dinner. Mrs. Gale,
wife of a small clothier who "doesn't keep a servant but does
the work of the house herself," hates the Irishman Malone for
his arrogant incivility. "More bread," he cries out to her.

> Mrs. Gale offered the loaf.
> "Cut it, woman," said her guest; and the "woman" cut it
> accordingly. Had she followed her inclinations, she would
> have cut the parson also; her Yorkshire soul revolted absolutely
> from his manner of command. [I, chap. 1, 5]

Malone's impious arrogance marks him as a stranger to Yorkshire. In *Shirley*, Charlotte Brontë attributes to Yorkshire a
traditional mutual respect and commonality among classes;
allowing for a rough independence but also for a fixed hierar-
chy, this commonality is posited in the novel as the basis on
which harmony, a pious, vital community life, might be regained. Moreover, this once extant harmony, although partly
violated in the novel by the Yorkshire people themselves, is
most crudely violated by any number of outsiders. Prominent
in this alien invasion, the curates expose themselves as un-
worthy by their crass intolerance, their boorishness, their
scorn for the claims of human moral equality. Brontë point-
edly underlines, in the opening scene, the false distinction
between servant and guest. The quotation marks around
"woman" indicate, as well, that she intends us to notice, beyond the false distinctions of class, the equally false distinctions between the sexes. Far from an irrelevancy, then, the
curates dramatize one aspect of the external threat to Yorkshire and, chiefly, a certain male self-centeredness, a pervasive
male chauvinism (to use our language).[49]

But while the initial exchange between Malone and Mrs.

---

49. The curates' dual function is most fully (and humorously) portrayed
in vol. 1, chap. 15, which Brontë titles "Mr. Donne's Exodus."

Gale introduces one of the novel's main themes, it also reveals
how the novel will go wrong: it isn't that Malone commands
her as much as "his manner of command" that irks Mrs. Gale.
Malone is a bad master—what one wants, the novel comes to
argue, are true masters. But this uncomfortable conclusion is
merely a suggestion in the opening scenes, a small part of a
picture that, with the introduction of the Reverend Helstone,
becomes enlarged to include the full setting of the novel.
Helstone introduces the spirited Yorkshire gentry, the old
parsons and landowners. To this extent he contrasts admirably with the curates, as Brontë intends. But she intends him as
well to represent one of the fatal flaws of the old Yorkshire
which have brought it to the present state of disharmony. If
Yorkshire must be purged of alien ways, it must also purge
itself of oppressive social forms. Helstone, a rock of the older
generation, stands, like Sir Thomas in *Mansfield Park*, for a
solidity become rigid and unequal to the demands of a vital
continuity. Like Sir Thomas a careless and inadequate guardian, he is the key figure of wounding male authority in the
novel.

In the opening chapter Helstone also introduces the working class. He tells the curates of his run-in with the out-of-
work Antinomian weaver Mike Hartley, and of Hartley's vision signifying " 'bloodshed and civil conflict' " (I, chap. 1, 11).
Helstone's errand, moreover, is to muster one of the curates to
sit with the millowner Robert Moore, waiting alone in his
counting house for a shipment of "frames and shears" (I, chap.
1, 12). With this dangerous task introduced and Malone dis-
patched, we begin to glimpse the political intentions of the
novel.

Malone finds Moore locked in his mill, slightly annoyed by
the Irishman's intrusion on his solitary vigil. Nonetheless, in
the tenseness of waiting, the men eat and talk—almost immediately of marriage. "They have assigned me every mar-
riageable single woman by turns in the district," Moore observes.

"On what grounds this gossip rests, God knows. I visit nowhere—I seek female society about as assiduously as you do, Mr Malone. If ever I go to Whinbury, it is only to give Sykes or Pearson a call in their counting-house; where our discussions run on . . . other things than courtships, establish-ments, dowries: the cloth we can't sell, the hands we can't employ, the mills we can't run . . . fill our hearts . . . to the tolerably complete exclusion of such figments as love-making, &c."

"I go along with you completely, Moore. If there is one notion I hate more than another, it is that of marriage: I mean marriage in the vulgar sense, as a mere matter of sentiment . . . some fantastic tie of feeling—humbug! But an advantageous connexion, such as can be formed in consonance with dignity of views, and permanency of solid interests, is not so bad—eh?" [I, chap. 2, 22]

Elsewhere in the novel the identification of marriage with the world of women is qualified; but the critical juxtaposition here of selling and its self-serving values and marriage damns Moore and Malone, locked up as they are, literally and figura-tively, in the countinghouse. That Moore should be merce-nary in his dealings with his workers is not surprising. We expect as much. But Brontë insists that Moore's subordination of all to money expresses a deeper flaw, and that we should see Moore, as George Eliot asks us to see Lydgate, as a man whose spots of commonness betray a debilitating perversion of value. Moore, like the curates, and like Helstone and Yorke, sins against piety—that is, against the just claims of respect made by others, against the claims of a caring morality, and against the inner claims of his own self for emotional fulfillment through human relationships. His heart is full of business, he is obsessed with "Forward!," as Charlotte Brontë says, to the "exclusion of such figments as love-making." If this obsession leads him "not sufficiently [to] care when the new inventions threw the old work-people out of employ" (I, chap. 2, 29), it also leads him to succumb fully, out of the logic of the charac-ter he has forged for himself, to the crass motivation in sexual relations which Malone advises. Shirley reprimands him with a wounding accuracy when, near the end of the novel, she remarks of his failed proposal: " 'You spoke like a brigand who demanded my purse, rather than like a lover who asked my heart' " (II, chap. 30, 236). Piety expresses a social reverence for the sanctity of other human lives: in its arrogant subordination of all to the interests of self the mercenary male world violates community. This is the feminist message of *Shirley*. Its aim, in contrast, is to assert passion, passionate feeling and passionate care, as the necessary social basis of community and personal fulfillment.

The opening chapters of the novel hold out the possibility that this intention might be realized in the full context of the society Charlotte Brontë has ambitiously chosen to depict. But the novel develops unevenly. Its treatment of class conflict, as I have already argued, is in the last analysis strictly conventional: the history of Luddism is told from "above." I do not mean to suggest that the novel for this reason fails to achieve unity. Luddism, I believe, is thoroughly integrated into the novel, but Brontë fails imaginatively to render working-class life. In Lukács's sense, the working-class characters lack typicality. In contrast, the novel's treatment of single women, to which I now turn, is unsurpassed in English fiction of the Industrial Revolution.

Shirley shows what it means to be a woman in a male world. The subjection of women is well illustrated in the grim, frightening story of the marriage of the martial Reverend Helstone to Mary Cave. The object of the devoted passion of Helstone's antithesis, the Radical squire Hiram Yorke, Mary Cave is "a girl with the face of a Madonna; a girl of living marble; stillness personified" (I, chap. 4, 54). She is, that is to say, an extreme instance of that wan Victorian ideal, the retiring, respectful, repressed woman, a lovelier Fanny Price. Caring less for her than does Yorke, and thus "more master of her and himself," Helstone succeeds in marrying her (I, chap. 4, 54). But, as Charlotte Brontë gingerly puts it, "Nature never intended Mr Helstone to make a very good husband, espe-

cially to a quiet wife" (I, chap. 4, 54). This is a generous
assessment. Wholly self-centered, arrogant, insensitive,
Helstone marries his wife only to forget her. "He thought, so
long as a woman was silent, nothing ailed her, and she wanted
nothing" (I, chap. 4, 54). The notion of an actual human
relationship with a woman seems to Helstone virtually a contradiction in terms. "*His* wife, after a year or two, was of no
great importance to him in any shape; and when she one day,
as he thought, suddenly—for he had scarcely noticed her
decline—but as others thought gradually, took her leave of
him and of life . . . he felt his bereavement—who shall say how
little?" (I, chap. 4, 55). Mary Cave is a victim of a male insen-
sitivity the novel views as deep and pervasive; her death is
intended to be instructive, a lesson and a foreshadowing. It
sets the tone for the discussion of marriage in the novel, and
echoes in the oppressive neglect Helstone bestows on
Caroline. In a larger sense, Helstone's neglect is a single instance of the broader social neglect of women which the novel
attacks.

Although the opening chapters put marriage forward as
containing values opposite to those of business, and although
marriage is reaffirmed at the novel's close, the viability of
marriage is put to serious question in the book—more serious
than in any other novel of the years of industrialization that I
am aware of. The vapid or painful or dreary marriages Austen
shows us, for example, are rarely discussed by the marriage-
able younger generation or taken as warnings of what might
come. Happily-ever-after is assumed and unquestioned—
certainly by those who still have choice. *Jane Eyre*, too, despite
its social insistence on sexual equality, settles for marriage
without much airing of doubt. But in *Shirley* marriages are, in
the first place, more than unhappy: as in the cases of Mary
Cave and Mrs. Pryor, they can be either literally or emotionally deadly. And these chastening examples function in the
novel as more than silent, ironic shadows—as, say, the Bennets' marriage does in *Pride and Prejudice*—but as explicit, ex-

amined warnings. Helstone and Mrs. Pryor both baldly translate their experience into advice. Both Caroline and Shirley
are made fully conscious that the examples behind them are of
unhappy marriages. As well, the novel looks on marriage as
possibly an exception, as an eventuality that by no means
comes to save all women from their social uselessness in the
male world, and one that may not come to save Caroline.
Caroline's long introspection about her life begins in earnest
when, her innocent assumption that Robert Moore would
naturally marry her having proved naive, she confronts a future devoid of either purposeful work or satisfying emotional
relationships. Stunned by the collapse of her romantic day-
dreams, Caroline looks with new eyes on the lives of the un-
married, seeking in them some help for her own. She resolves
to visit, and learn from, the old maids Miss Mann and Miss
Ainley.

It is significant that, before taking Caroline to the homes of
Miss Mann and Miss Ainley, Brontë pauses to remark on the
typically casual derision Moore had on occasion cast on Miss
Mann. After one visit Miss Mann had paid his sister Hortense,
Moore is described as having joined Caroline in his garden and
"amused himself with comparing fair youth—delicate and
attractive—with shrivelled eld, livid and loveless, and in jest-
ingly repeating to a smiling girl the vinegar discourse of a
cankered old maid" (I, chap. 10, 197). Caroline's newly serious
consideration of single women is set, then, in the context both
of her failed hopes and of the hard mockery of the male world.
The portraits of these two women, one uglier than the
other—Miss Ainley so ugly that "all but peculiarly well-
disciplined minds were apt to turn from her with annoyance"
(I, chap. 10, 201)—are masterpieces of their kind. Their
power, too, comes from their rarity—the shrunken life that a
woman's ugliness or poverty may promise is rarely exposed in
the nineteenth-century English novel. Here these women, un-
attractive, single, lonely, are not only faced—the word seems
unusually apt—but given a central structural role in the de-

veloping argument of the novel. The two old maids are important because they make us see concretely the living opposites
of the pleasing women Helstone likes to toy with; but, even
more, because their resigned gentility—real and admirable
though it is—does not satisfy. In following their lead,
Caroline, still only in the early stages of her depression, finds
occasional "gleams of satisfaction" but "neither health of body
nor continued peace of mind" (I, chap. 10, 205).

It is against the background of the old maids Miss Mann and
Miss Ainley, of Helstone's bitter opposition to marriage, of
Moore's immersion in his contest with his workmen to the
exclusion of Caroline and her expectations of love, of
Caroline's consequent resolve to find some work to fill her
life—it is against this background that Caroline and Shirley
take their long walk on Nunnely Common. Their walk and its
setting bring to mind the relationship between Fanny Price
and Mary Crawford. The comparison shows continuity of
themes but also profound differences. The walk Fanny ad-
mires, for example, is an artificial stretch of bushes, classic in
its domestication of nature. But in *Shirley* the two women do
not so much admire as embrace or throw their identities into
the stretch of a whole valley below them, a valley at whose
center grows "the sole remnant of antique British forest" (I,
chap. 12, 230). This is a nature with its own temptations,
which Brontë is on occasion apt to worship as a solace from
and a source of energy for the much more constricted—but yet
the human—round of social relationships. The range of conversation matches its setting in the same way that Fanny's
carefully genteel observation matches the planned symmetry
of her favorite walk. In *Shirley*, that is, the conversation is
truly exploratory—Caroline and Shirley consider unconventional (wild) possibilities: whether men are inevitably different
from women, whether marriage is advisable, whether sisterhood is not more certain and satisfying than the dangerous
improbability of marriage.

This latter possibility is the first stressed. Caroline and

Shirley are both perfectly conscious that they can behave and observe together in a way they could not were men present. Sisterhood makes possible kinds of intimacy heterosexual relations do not offer. But while this view, more intently argued later in the novel, is firmly noted, the pull of conversation between Caroline and Shirley is toward some sense of the possibilities of a loving relationship between men and women. "I often wonder," Caroline muses,

> "whether most men resemble my uncle in their domestic relations; whether it is necessary to be new and unfamiliar to them in order to seem agreeable . . . ; whether it is impossible to their natures to retain a constant interest and affection for those they see every day."
>
> "I don't know. . . . But . . . if I were convinced that they are necessarily and universally different from us—fickle, soon petrifying, unsympathizing—I would never marry. I should not like to find out that what I loved did not love me. . . ." [I, chap. 12, 235]

The assumption of constancy and abiding emotional commitment in women and its opposite in men is a characteristic emphasis of the novel. It is the absence of the woman's sensibility in the realms of power that has caused the violation of community. But the danger, for women, of their difference from men is that it can draw them into an imprisoning marriage. If the married woman loses the love of her husband—a likely prospect, both women say—she must stick it out—"A terrible thought!—it suffocates me!" Shirley protests. For this reason both women suspect their tendency to make exception, before marriage, of the men they love; and thus Shirley's conclusion: "'I don't think we should trust to what they call passion at all, Caroline'" (I, chap. 12, 236). Yet Shirley follows these words immediately with a description—though we are unaware of it at the time—of Louis Moore, and declares, "'Indisputably, a great, good, handsome man is the first of created things.'" Caroline meets this inconsistent assertion of man's superiority with a dubiousness Shirley confidently refutes: "'Nothing ever charms me more than when I meet my

superior.'" "'Did you ever meet him?'" Caroline asks. "'I
should be glad to see him any day. . . . What frets me is, that
when I try to esteem, I am baffled: when religiously inclined,
there are but false gods to adore'" (I, chap. 12, 238).

This dramatically frank exploration of the differences between and the relations of the sexes, developed more fully but
not essentially altered later in the novel, brings Caroline and
Shirley to a number of basic but apparently incompatible insights: that women can give each other emotional satisfaction
unobtainable from men; that marriage, because it definitively
limits freedom, may suffocate; that passionate love, nevertheless, promises the greatest satisfaction; and that integral to
such a love is the submission of woman to the mastery of man.

Today this final point is difficult to swallow; much has been
said to soft-pedal it and save Charlotte Brontë's feminism from
a conclusion we do not approve. But I think the point is ines-
capable and integral to the novel. It is Mrs. Gale's objection to
Malone applied emphatically to sexual relations. It has its
equivalent in Shirley's—and I think without any doubt Charlotte Brontë's—political philosophy. And it is upheld by the
final outcome of the plot. Our coming to terms with this point
is not made easier by the fact that Shirley sounds exactly like
many women in D. H. Lawrence's fiction—strong women
who cannot find satisfaction because they cannot find a real
man. In Lawrence phallic superiority is supported by the
implicit—and in many places explicit—argument that modern
society has sapped men of their vital energy, and that in seeking this energy in men, women recognize a failure in modern
life that must be universally grasped before any progress toward a richer social life, and toward satisfying sexual relations, can be attained. This argument applies in Shirley: the
damage inflicted by a mercenary male world on social
relations—relations between the classes and the sexes—and on
individuals is as palpable in Shirley as in any of Lawrence's
novels. Nonetheless it cannot help but be disconcerting that
the demand for mastery as the clinching element of an alterna-

tive value system should come from such a woman as Shirley, and should come despite the novel's emphatic condemnation of man's oppression of woman and its clear statement that the danger of marriage comes from the inequality of power it grants men and women. That in this novel Brontë considers and rejects as valuable but inadequate the posited alternatives to passionate love between men and women in marriage seems, at the very least, honest. It is the final turn in the argument that leaves one surprised and uncomfortable. Be that as it may, I think it betrays the novel's honesty to try to argue away its uncomfortable conclusion. At best, we can grant the novel its ambiguities. The alternatives to passionate love, as well as its dangers, are not taken in the novel as far as they might be, but neither are they fudged: Miss Mann, Miss Ainley, the marriages of Helstone and Mrs. Pryor, the advantages of sisterhood, and the freedom of remaining single could not be more plainly presented or more forcefully acknowledged. Caroline tells Shirley that their sisterly relation offers "affection that no passion can ultimately outrival" (I, chap. 14, 289). Mrs. Pryor bitterly warns Caroline that no marriage is ever "'wholly happy. Two people can never literally be as one. . . . Let all the singles be satisfied with their freedom'" (II, chap. 21, 68).

But all of this having been said, the novel still offers no substitute for passionate love between men and women. Louis Moore's appearance late in the novel, cumbersome as it may be as a piece of narrative management, is yet crucial to the book's finally romantic argument. Brontë's trouble with point of view once Louis is on the scene and her sudden leap into an unabashedly inflated rhetoric qualify Louis's unquestionably pivotal role in the plot, but they do no more. Louis is essential because he differs from all the other men in the novel. It is important that he is poor, powerless, and consequently untainted by the self-seeking impiety of his brother; but more important is his positive example as a man for whom passionate care is primary from the start, and who does not need to learn that it *should* be so. His personal power is neither warped by nor expressed through the arrogance of social or political power but derives from his knowledge of himself and the inner force of feeling. In contrast his brother Robert must suffer exile and a kind of death before he can be reborn pious and fit to marry Caroline.

Louis, the true master Shirley seeks, understands what he must do: "'However kindly the hand—if it is feeble, it cannot bend Shirley; and she must be bent: it cannot curb her, and she must be curbed'" (II, chap. 29, 226). Because Louis's appearance at Fieldhead coincides with the appearance of other suitors for Shirley's hand, Shirley carries on a kind of dual resistance: on one hand, a resistance to any merely prudent marriage; on the other, a resistance to Louis's power over her. But in refusing others, Shirley establishes the basis of her preference for Louis. She won't marry the eminently eligible Sir Philip Nunnely, she says, because he is "'not my master,'" though she *will* marry "'a man I shall feel it impossible not to love, and very possible to fear'" (II, chap. 31, 255–56). Oddly, this struggle ends, when Shirley and Louis finally declare their love to each other, with Shirley's startling exclamation "'And are we equal then, sir? Are we equal at last?'" (II, chap. 36, 336).

Shirley means here, as far as I can tell, that marriage will make the penniless Louis her equal as well as that they will now share an emotional reciprocity. But her words are at best confusing. The truth is, I think, that Charlotte Brontë felt with equal strength the oppression of women in her society and the need for passionate fulfillment through sexual submission. The need for passionate fulfillment is realized in the marriages or romances she makes happen in her novels. The need for a full life for women as for men leads to the demand for equality—but this demand is not compatible with the need for a master, and necessarily Charlotte Brontë does not manage a reconciliation of these demands in any of her novels. The discrepancy between the two demands is especially clear in *Shirley* because the available alternatives to marriage form an essential part of the novel's social analysis. Ironically, exploration of alternatives to marriage reinforces marriage as the only satisfying fulfillment because, in *Shirley*, Brontë is baffled in her search for an alternative that might actually serve. The *need* for alternatives is seen very clearly; but the alternatives considered fall far short of the need to be filled.

Compare, for example, the passion with which Brontë describes disappointment in love and the feebleness of her suggestions for other means of life. (Unconventional as the novel is, it does not go so far as to contemplate employment for a married woman.) Here Caroline first realizes Robert will not marry her:

> You have held out your hand for an egg, and fate put into it a scorpion. Show no consternation: close your fingers firmly upon the gift; let it sting through your palm. Never mind: in time, after your hand and arm have swelled and quivered long with torture, the squeezed scorpion will die, and you will have learned the great lesson how to endure without a sob.   [I, chap. 7, 114]

The bitter emptiness that is the residue of such experience demands some activity, some social role for women, "'something absorbing and compulsory,'" as Caroline says, "'to fill my head and hands, and to occupy my thoughts.'" But this notion of trade or profession, though important, is still finally mere filler. Caroline's plea that "'single women should have more to do—better chances of interesting and profitable occupation than they possess now'" (II, chap. 22, 82) should be read next to Robert Moore's remark that "'so long as I can be active, so long as I can strive, so long, in short, as my hands are not tied, it is impossible for me to be depressed'" (I, chap. 16, 320).[50] In juxtaposition these two passages demonstrate

50. Cf. these remarks from one of Brontë's letters to W. S. Williams: "Believe me, teachers may be hard-worked, ill-paid, and despised, but the girl who stays at home doing nothing is worse off than the hardest-wrought and worst-paid drudge of a school. Whenever I have seen, not merely in humble but in affluent homes, families of daughters sitting waiting to be married, I have pitied them from my heart" (quoted in Clement K. Shorter, *The Brontës: Life and Letters* [2 vols.; New York: Haskell House, 1969 (1908)], Letter 358, July 3, 1849, II, 58).

the crucial need for real work for women. But despite the fact that it is perfectly clear the single women in the novel find themselves precisely with their hands tied, unable to strive or be active, and face therefore a depression Moore surely cannot imagine, the passionate language that describes disappointment is not matched by the weak "women should have more to do" or by the one occupation for women the novel takes seriously—the position of governess. Although the likelihood that marriage will turn sour is amply recognized, and although the blatant injustice of women's social irrelevance is equally recognized, Brontë is baffled by the lack of prospects for women in the dramatized society.

Nevertheless she is not simply beaten back to an acceptance of marriage. It is perhaps impossible to imagine truly the fears and restraints Charlotte Brontë had to contend with in reflecting on sexual relations. What is more certain is that she did not seriously entertain the possibility of sexual relations between men and women outside of marriage. Marriage was therefore powerfully attractive, especially because it offered not simply sex but a whole relationship—the essential possibility of fulfilling, mutual, passionate love. For Brontë, nothing in the life of old maids and no trade or profession offers as much. Moreover, the disparagement of marriage comes in the novel from those who either deny the value of personal relations—Moore before his change of heart, and Helstone—or from those who, like Mrs. Pryor, profess an extreme pessimism and an extreme conservatism of feeling. In neither case do these critics put before us an inviting example of a possible way of life: Brontë never suggests that Robert or Louis would do well to emulate Helstone or that Shirley or Caroline would do well to emulate Mrs. Pryor. The novel's final affirmation is therefore partly a defeat but also partly a triumph. At the very least, the novel affirms marriage after a searching analysis of its flaws and dangers, and of alternative possibilities.

As much cannot be said of the novel's political resolution. The novel's gestures toward an analysis of class conflict are not followed through. For example, Caroline's mild objection,

early in the novel, to Robert Moore's manner with his workmen appears to have Brontë's assent and to establish an initial
step toward clarification of the issues. Caroline protests: "'I
cannot help thinking it unjust to include all poor working
people under the general and insulting name of "the mob," and
continually to think of them and treat them haughtily'" (I,
chap. 6, 101). This criticism is not bad, as far as it goes. The
phrase Caroline uses is not the wholly inaccurate "the poor"
but the somewhat better "poor working people." And the objection she makes to Moore's peremptory resort to "the mob"
is telling. But as the novel develops and the conflict between
classes intensifies, Caroline's statement gets turned on its head
in Shirley's flashy testament of landed right: "'At present I am
no patrician, nor do I regard the poor around me as plebeians;
but if once they violently wrong me or mine, and then pre-
sume to dictate to us, I shall quite forget pity for their wretch-
edness and respect for their poverty, in scorn of their ignorance and wrath at their insolence'" (I, chap. 14, 293). Brontë's
posited Yorkshire harmony does not survive these words very
well. The "ignorance" to which Shirley refers is, presumably,
the workers' ignorance of their place. "'If once the poor gather
and rise in the form of the mob,'" Shirley warns, "'I shall turn
against them as an aristocrat'" (I, chap. 14, 293). Caroline's
objections are thus brusquely set aside: "the poor" becomes
standard usage and the elision from "the poor" to "the mob" is
more peremptory than ever. The workers are not a mob so
long as they behave with due deference, accept Shirley's charity and her pity, and make do.

One can't say of this position that it represents a searching
analysis. *Shirley's* judgment of the workers and their cause
simply reflects the class prejudices of its author. If this is not
altogether a surprise, it is still important to say that this *is* the
case, and to note its consequences for the novel. Charlotte
Brontë's inability to imagine the workers at their work or to
realize work relationships in the novel may be a just measure
of ideological possibility at the time she wrote; but it means

nonetheless that the novel takes up Luddism without ever addressing the real issues at stake. Surely one could have expected the novel's judgment that "misery generates hate" (I, chap. 2, 30) to have served as a perspective on Luddism, but it does not. Once Shirley is on the scene, Brontë quickly drops Caroline's (and perhaps her own) reservations about industrial capitalism: the workers become abstracted into the definitive category "the poor" and then, easily, into a stance of fixed ideological menace as "the mob."[51] From *this* perspective the workers' rising against Moore becomes the sole issue, the mitigating circumstance of their misery being forgotten. The rising is taken virtually as a breach of decorum, and certainly as the working-class equivalent of Moore's impious arrogance. Having in this way abstracted and distorted the actual conflict, the novel offers as meliorative a thoroughly abstract resolution: a return, by worker and owner, to Yorkshire pieties, specifically to due respect between the classes. Moore's change of heart, if matched by a change of heart by the workers, will heal the social rupture and regain Yorkshire harmony. But this resolution ignores the original cause of conflict, the imposition of laissez faire, and therefore is not viable. Moore may have changed his boorish regard for his workers, but his machines remain.

The novel's romantic resolution, more convincing for the reasons I have already stated, nonetheless also displays this kind of abstraction. Louis Moore's exceptional male passion may allow him to master Shirley, but his introduction effectively avoids a romantic resolution *within* the world of the novel. Louis is a man without a social place; he comes, like the

51. In 1831 Henry Hetherington wrote in his *Penny Papers for the People*, the predecessor to his more famous *Poor Man's Guardian*, that "the middling classes will never wish the poor and the despised 'mob,' as even *they* call the *working classes*, to have equal power with themselves" (quoted by Asa Briggs in his introduction to William Lovett and John Collins, *Chartism: A New Organization of the People* [Leicester: Leicester University Press, 1969 (first published London, 1840)], p. 8).

circus in *Hard Times*, from outside the landed-industrial society *Shirley* depicts; his values, therefore, have no social equivalent. Neither landowner, industrialist, nor worker, Louis descends on Fieldhead pretty much as *deus ex machina*. Moreover, what Louis ideologically imports, and what Caroline and Shirley finally accept, is simply marriage. The "woman question" is resolved, like class conflict, without any social change. Caroline and Shirley gain neither trade, profession, nor any other activity: they assume, in the end, the same role Caroline would have assumed had she married Robert Moore in the early pages of the novel.[52]

III

I began my discussion of *Shirley* by saying that the problem both Charlotte Brontë and Jane Austen address in all their fiction is: How, under what circumstances of character and society, can fulfillment be achieved? This problem divides into two parts: What qualities are necessary in the individual for her to realize fulfillment? And what social circumstances will nurture individual fulfillment? My discussion of *Pride and Prejudice* and *Jane Eyre* in the previous chapter and of *Mansfield Park* and *Shirley* in this one suggests how Austen and Brontë answer these questions.

Pride and Prejudice and *Jane Eyre* stress necessary qualities in the individual. What we are shown is a process of growth by

---

52. We can gauge the momentousness of Shirley's decision to marry Louis if we consider the legal position of women in marriage at the time. According to Françoise Basch,

the doctrine of the union of man and woman amounted to placing all the wife's possessions at the disposal of the husband, in return for which he was supposed to guarantee her his protection and provide for her needs. Everything belonging to the wife at the moment of marriage, chattels and real estate, became, with few exceptions, the husband's property, as well as anything she might acquire later on: annuities, personal income, gifts and emoluments. [*Relative Creatures: Victorian Women in Society and the Novel*, trans. Anthony Rudolf (New York: Schocken Books, 1974), pp. 19–20] means of which individual qualities are strengthened and shaped as aspiration translates, through experience and trial, into achievement. In both novels aspiration exceeds achievement, although we are convinced that the achieved resolutions promise fulfillment. Elizabeth Bennet's unqualified assertion, at the beginning of *Pride and Prejudice*, of woman's right to a marriage based exclusively on love expresses a progressive aspiration the novel qualifies by reference to and yet successfully merges with the notion of marriage as a social contract. Jane Eyre's more radical aspirations extend Elizabeth Bennet's under circumstances more demanding of individual energy and perseverance. Jane, through dynamism and work, gains a marriage of remarkable equality;[53] but her yearning for an active life in the wide world is not achieved. Both novels, then, show us their society insofar as the individual careers traced express typical conditions of social life.

But in *Mansfield Park* and *Shirley* this element of typicality, in Lukács's sense, is noticeably weaker. The reason is that these novels no longer consider mainly the question: What qualities are necessary in the individual for her to realize a full life? but are intent on the relation between that question and its complement: What social circumstances will nurture individual fulfillment? In both novels the particular social place from within which both authors write is seen by them as under threat, a threat much less noticeable in the earlier novels. Observing the life they prize as threatened, both novelists in a sense retreat into it: neither author, in these novels, expresses the totality of social relations or what Leslie Stephen calls "the social movement." Moreover, Elizabeth Bennet's and Jane Eyre's impulses toward freedom come to be

53. "If one had to pick the decisive moment in English literature when feminine emancipation became a literary fact of primary importance . . . we would have to settle on . . . Charlotte Brontë's *Jane Eyre*, a landmark in Victorian literature inasmuch as, for the first time, here was a fictional woman confronting fictional man on equal terms" (Amaury de Riencourt, *Sex and Power in History* [New York: David McKay, 1974], p. 324).

seen as themselves part of what threatens social stability. It is as if, in *Mansfield Park* and *Shirley*, Austen and Brontë became suddenly afraid of their own feelings, and saw these feelings objectified in monstrous social forms—in the London morality of Mary Crawford, in the rebelliousness of the working class. If *Pride and Prejudice* and *Jane Eyre* express women's aspirations for a full life, they are less concerned to examine the social agency said to establish that fulfillment: both novels are satisfied with the structure of courtship. *Mansfield Park* and *Shirley*, in contrast, assess the viability of social forms, their ability to give substance to aspiration. But if the demands of *Pride and Prejudice* and of *Jane Eyre* extend into the later novels, the later novels find in the worlds they observe only perverse or dangerous social innovations: Mary Crawford and the Luddites represent a newfangledness to which neither author can assent. But neither can Jane Austen or Charlotte Brontë imagine any new social agency that might enable fulfillment. Consequently both novels retreat into abstract affirmations of a conservative harmony: the estate Mansfield Park and Yorkshire. Rather than express the total life of their era through an active engagement with its history, both novels instead impose on that history a fixed ideological message; instead of typicality both novels fall back on class-bound narratives. *Mansfield Park* and *Shirley* enact, in different ways, two versions of a social dead end; they show us how, in the absence of a vision of social change, aspirations for fulfillment were stifled.

Having said this, I want to point again to the differences between the books. *Mansfield Park*, written at the time of and in the spirit of the counterrevolution of the 1810s, suppresses the contradictions in the society and the contradictions between the progressive demands of women for a full life and the general social retrenchment. Having maintained from the start that the individual is unthinkable without society, Austen naturally sacrifices the individual's desire for fulfillment to the demands of social stability. Without social stability no civilized relations are, in her view, possible; consequently retrenchment, for Austen, is a positive social step toward the maintenance of real value. But Brontë, who does not join the individual and society in the same way, and leaves open the possibility that a given society may not serve the just interests of the individual, dramatizes in *Shirley* the social contradictions she hopes to resolve. For this reason *Shirley* is partly a triumph and for this reason it does not represent simply retrenchment. Even where the novel is weakest, in its treatment of Luddism, it exhibits, albeit from the point of view of Brontë's class, the effective social contradictions. In its treatment of women, the novel exposes contradictions fully, although it does not approach a revolutionary resolution. It does not contemplate any future that might fulfill the genuine aspirations of the present in a realizable social development.

Of course it is easy to list possibilities in retrospect; but what seems possible to us must have seemed to Charlotte Brontë as visionary, or as a millennial projection. We know that Charlotte Brontë was in no way attracted by millennial possibilities, and probably considered even the revolutionary future she so much hungered for to gain her own liberation as a future that would not come to be. She was for this reason all the more insistent that the deep contradictions of everyday life which she set loose in her fiction find an everyday resolution, an imminent outcome. This insistence on livable resolutions, on what she could see to be possible, for her, in 1848, was her special contribution to her culture and her art. What *Shirley* shows us, after we have named its failures, is what a middle-class observer as clear-eyed as Charlotte Brontë could, in the 1840s, see as possible. She could see what the demands of the decade were; she could not see how to enact them.

CHAPTER FIVE

Correspondences

THE Industrial Revolution transformed every aspect of English life. Although this fact is obvious and no one disputes it, there is little agreement about the relation between this process of transformation and people's ideas or values or attitudes. Walter Houghton, in *The Victorian Frame of Mind*, asks: "What corresponds in the intellectual world to the establishment of bourgeois industrial society?" and answers: "Nothing."[1] Implicit in this extreme response is the notion that, at that time, change occurred dramatically and initially in social development but more slowly and later in art, or, in the bare Marxist version, that there was a lag between development of structure and that of superstructure. The problem with this formulation is well illustrated by another of Houghton's sentences: "The radical transition in the human mind was less apparent at first than that in society, but sensitive observers were soon aware that the traditional framework of thought was breaking down."[2] But since "the human mind" is not an abstraction and can be found only in a human person,

1. Walter Houghton, *The Victorian Frame of Mind, 1830–1870* (New Haven: Yale University Press, 1957), p. 9.
2. Ibid., p. 8.

and since people live in society, where are we to go to find "the human mind" if not in society? The separation between mind and society Houghton casually offers, as well as his notion of a fixed cause and effect, belies the complex process of social development in which idea and enactment make up a whole.

A useful hypothesis about the relation between material history and consciousness cannot proceed along the lines Houghton implies. Besides, we have in fact an answer to Houghton's question—it is *Pride and Prejudice* or *The Condition of the Working Class in England* or the factory system or the Crystal Palace. Houghton looks for, perhaps, Joyce's *Ulysses* or Stravinsky's *Rite of Spring* or Chaplin's *Modern Times;* when he doesn't find it he concludes that "nothing" corresponds in consciousness to industrial capitalism. This is not very helpful. Rather than look for a development in ideology that *should* occur, it seems to me more fruitful to try to establish how the work that was actually produced reflects and reflects on the Industrial Revolution. For the novelists who wrote during the Industrial Revolution necessarily wrote out of the experience of social transformation that actually occurred, *and* in response to it. I have tried to demonstrate some connections between political economy and the novel, and to examine *Mansfield Park* and *Shirley* as examples of historical response. I would like to add to what I have written, and to draw my discussion to a close, by studying correspondences between the novel and courtship, crime, and the crowd.

I

Some critics have said that Jane Austen's novels represent the climax of eighteenth-century fiction while others have seen her work as inaugurating the practice of nineteenth-century fiction.[3] The dates of composition of her novels, to mention

3. E.g., "*Pride and Prejudice* shows no sharp cleavage from the structure of the later and more finished examples of the eighteenth century novel"

nothing else, suggest that both judgments may be accurate: she wrote during the pivotal transition within the longer process of the Industrial Revolution. This experience of transition—after the great work of the eighteenth-century novelists but before the flowering of Victorian fiction; during the expansive stage of industrial capitalism but before the bitter decades between the campaigns against Napoleon and construction of the Crystal Palace—this experience of transition gives her work its special character. Of course Austen did not know what was to come after her; but we can see in retrospect that the taut formal and thematic solutions that give her works the dimensions of classics come out of this experience of a pivotal transition.

Ian Watt says that Jane Austen "faces more squarely than Defoe . . . the social and moral problems raised by economic individualism and the middle class quest for improved status; she follows Richardson in basing her novels on marriage and especially on the proper feminine role in the matter; and her ultimate picture of the proper norms of the social system is similar to that of Fielding although its application to the characters and their situation is in general more serious and discriminating."[4]

Austen's advantage over Defoe, for one, was both that she wrote after him and that the social developments he saw at a rudimentary stage had matured: Austen wrote not only after Defoe but just after Adam Smith. Her work then represents the climax of the eighteenth-century novel in that she brings to

---

(Harrison R. Steeves, *Before Jane Austen: The Shaping of the English Novel in the Eighteenth Century* [New York: Holt, Rinehart & Winston, 1965], p. 346). Ian Watt sees her novels as the "climax" of the eighteenth-century novel, whereas A. Walton Litz says that "with *Pride and Prejudice* Jane Austen bid farewell to her early life and to the eighteenth century" (Watt, *The Rise of the Novel: Studies in Defoe, Richardson, and Fielding* [Berkeley: University of California Press, 1957], p. 298; Litz, "Into the Nineteenth Century: *Pride and Prejudice*," in *Twentieth-Century Interpretations of "Pride and Prejudice*," ed. E. Rubinstein [Englewood Cliffs, N.J.: Prentice-Hall, 1969], p. 59).
   4. Watt, *Rise of the Novel*, p. 298.

a new level and clarity the critical concerns of the English novel during the *whole stretch* of the Industrial Revolution. These concerns are the crucial interdependence of class mobility and individual aspiration, marriage, and "the proper norms of the social system." Austen presents, however, not only the classical formulation of these issues but also their classical formal shape and resolution. The form of her novels is itself a product of the experience of transition. "It is in the eighteenth century novel," Alistair Duckworth has written, "that the recurring pattern of Jane Austen's plots—the movement from a condition of initial security to a period of isolation and then to a final reinstatement in society—finds its origins." He defines this movement as a "circularity of plot structure."[5] The circle of the novels depends on the principle of reconciliation. But if the literary origin of the pattern of circularity is in the eighteenth-century novel, nonetheless the wholly satisfying reconciliations of, say, *Pride and Prejudice* depend on the social history that they express. For the effected reconciliations are not between what we might be able to isolate as autonomous formal elements but between love and money, trade and land, individual and society, self and other. The organizing principle of the novels—the principle of reconciliation—is embedded in the subject of the novels as well as in the point of view with which Austen grasps the contraries of her subject. It is this as it were immanent principle that finds outward expression in the structure of her plots. Hegel's definition of form as the shape of content seems especially apt in Austen's case.

The structure of reconciliation in Austen's work is illuminated by reference to the changing structure of courtship at the time she wrote. Outstanding in this changing structure is the sharpness of its contradictions. Borrowing Raymond Williams's categories, we can say that it is a structure in which

5. Alistair M. Duckworth, *The Improvement of the Estate: A Study of Jane Austen's Novels* (Baltimore: Johns Hopkins Press, 1971), pp. 10, 12.

residual and emergent elements have almost equal force. Relationships within the family before the eighteenth century are said to have been distinguished by considerable control by parents over their children, "most significantly perhaps," according to Michael Anderson, "over the timing of their marriages and over the choice of spouse."[6] Moreover, this seems to have been true among laborers, farmers, the city bourgeosie, and the country gentry. Under these circumstances courtship was subsumed under marriage and family. Marriage was an arrangement between families within a relatively stable social system; the assumed continuities of role and class stressed responsibility to family and community.

The census of 1851 revealed a drastically different pattern of social life. "In almost all large towns," Anderson says, "migrants from elsewhere outnumbered those born in the towns. This was particularly true of the cotton districts." The population of the towns was composed of a large number of teenagers who had either migrated to the towns by themselves or had been left in them as orphans. Less than 20 percent of the population of the towns had lived in the same house for over two years.[7]

One consequence of industrial capitalism, then, was a marked decrease of parental control over children. Among the urban working class the economic basis for this change was the children's ability to sustain themselves on their own earnings. But among the urban bourgeosie and the country gentry the same loosening of parental control is evident. This decline in the absolute authority of parents over children did not, however, result in the breakup of the family as much as in a transformation of familial bonds. Within families, at all social levels, new tensions of power and allegiance arose. One of the

6. Michael Anderson, *Family Structure in Nineteenth-Century Lancashire* (London: Cambridge University Press, 1971), pp. 141, 148.

7. Ibid., pp. 143, 141, 140, 127-32.

most dramatic causes of tension was the demand for love as a basis of marriage. The historian J. A. Banks writes:

> It cannot be denied that affection and love as a basis for marriage did not come into fashion at least until the end of the eighteenth century.... In the main, marriage for the middle and upper classes had been the concern of the parents whose one great responsibility was the choice of a suitable partner for a son or daughter. The aim here was to settle the child well in life and to enhance the wealth and dignity of the family.[8]

To say that marriage for love came into "fashion" is to misstate the case. It was not a question of a fashionable change in sensibility but of a profound change in social relationships. Probably, as well, this change occurred before the end of the eighteenth century. What we notice is a developing process. The question of value was in dispute, an emerging morality was being defined—as Mr. and Mrs. Bennet serve to tell us.[9] Austen mocks Mrs. Bennet for her crass single-mindedness (a boorishness Lady Catherine also displays) but judges Mr. Bennet's laissez faire as irresponsible. Here is Mary Astell's assessment of the matter as early as 1730:

> What do men propose to themselves in Marriage? What Qualifications do they look for in a Spouse? What will she bring? is the first Enquiry: How many Acres? Or how much ready Coin? Not that this is altogether an unnecessary Question, for Marriage without a Competency, that is, not only a bare Subsistence, but even a handsome and plentiful Provision, according to the Quality and Circumstances of the parties, is no very comfortable condition. They who marry for Love, as they call it, find time enough to repent their rash Folly.... But tho' an

8. J. A. Banks, *Prosperity and Parenthood: A Study of Family Planning among the Victorian Middle Class* (London: Routledge & Kegan Paul, 1954), p. 33.

9. Lawrence Stone, *The Family, Sex, and Marriage in England, 1500–1800*, abr. and rev. (Harmondsworth: Penguin Books, 1979), observes: "It is clear that the eighteenth century aristocracy and squirarchy were hopelessly torn in their sense of priorities and values in matrimonial projects and that no single or simple pattern will serve to explain the complex reality" (p. 212).

Estate is to be considered, it should not be the *Main*, much less the only Consideration; for Happiness does not depend on wealth.[10]

These sentences turn one against the other in an extraordinary niceness of discrimination. Happiness does not depend on wealth, but you can't be happy without wealth. To marry for Love is Folly; an Estate should not be the only Consideration. These discriminations anticipate the concerns of Richardson, Fanny Burney, and Jane Austen. But in Astell's account money looms larger than love. She indicates the situation in 1730, which is not wholly the situation of which Austen writes.

For by the end of the eighteenth century the changing roles of women under industrial and agricultural capitalism had further sharpened the contradiction between love and money. But the change in women's roles was complex. The working-class young woman gained through factory work a revolutionary independence. A teenage girl who could more or less keep herself might assert her own values against those of her family and maybe even her community. She might, especially, resist demands for any sort of merely utilitarian marriage. But the same girl would be just as likely to contribute to the family's upkeep. Her work, too, would be seen more as a job than as a career. The wage system that gave her independence also relegated her to the less desirable jobs and discriminated against her in pay. Moreover, the desire for upward mobility and respectability encouraged emulation of the middle class.

Paradoxically, the middle-class woman found herself in a privileged *dependence*. As a wife, the middle-class woman remained in a home that was now neither workplace nor a place that demanded the chores necessary before industrialization.

10. Mary Astell, *Some Reflections upon Marriage* (London, 1730), pp. 23–25, quoted in *The Family: Past and Present*, ed. Bernhard J. Stern (New York: D. Appleton-Century, 1938), p. 161.

Thus, the middle-class woman, stripped of economic function, found herself with very little to do. Potentially she may have been free to develop herself, perhaps intellectually, but she had precious few routes available to translate potential into social activity. The money the working-class woman could earn therefore raised the possibility of an equality severely qualified by the class system and by the contradictory expectations that that system encouraged. And the possibility of equality which the society now displayed to the middle-class woman was denied her because she was cut off from the world of work. By the end of the eighteenth century, then, the contraries that Mary Astell observed had intensified tension without creating clear new patterns of social relationships.

Some special conditions, finally, need to be noted among the landed gentry. Christopher Hill, in his "Clarissa Harlowe and Her Times,"[11] refers to H. J. Habakkuk's observation that in the early eighteenth century one finds "'an increasing subordination of marriage to the increase of landed wealth, at the expense of other motives for marriage.'" Among the upper classes, Habakkuk concludes, marriage was bent "'more systematically to the accumulation of landed wealth.'" Hill explains that Habakkuk traces this development to the settlements of 1660 and 1688, which left the landed class with their property but without power to check the growth of capitalism. The standards of wealth were set by those in trade. To defend their position the landed class resorted to concentration of estates as a means of accumulating capital. The consequence of this strategy was to establish the family unit, in its broadest sense, as the key institution of individual allegiance.[12]

Although, as J. A. Banks says, the dominant development

11. See chap. 14 of his *Puritanism and Revolution: Studies in Interpretation of the English Revolution of the Seventeenth Century* (London: Panther, 1968 [first published 1958]).

12. Hill, *Puritanism and Revolution*, p. 352. He refers to H. J. Habakkuk, "Marriage Settlements in the Eighteenth Century," *Transactions of the Royal Historical Society*, 1950, pp. 24–25.

in marital relations at the end of the eighteenth century was toward love as the basis for marriage, economic developments strengthened the demand for familial allegiance among the upper class. The nature of family life reinforced this transformed claim by the family on the allegiance of its young. The family historian Ronald Fletcher defines the family as "that association within which the earliest character-formation of individuals takes place—within which the earliest and deepest pattern of sentiments, attitudes, belief, ideals, and loyalties is established. The family is one of the most important agencies making for the *continuity of the social tradition*."[13] If we add Christopher Lasch's formulation that, "as the chief agency of socialization, the family reproduces cultural patterns in the individual,"[14] we can see why Burke valued the family so highly and saw it as a ballast of the state.[15] The family as an institution is, in this respect, by its nature conservative; it reproduces extant social relationships; it ensures continuity of social tradition.

Jane Austen values the family in much the same way as Burke does. But she is more attentive than he, or in any event

13. Ronald Fletcher, *Britain in the Sixties: The Family and Marriage* (Harmondsworth: Penguin Books, 1962), pp. 32-33; Fletcher's italics.

14. Christopher Lasch, "The Family and History," *New York Review of Books*, November 13, 1975, p. 33.

15. Analogies between family and state were not new. Lawrence Stone writes:

> The most direct and explicit link between political theory and family life occurs in John Locke's *Two Treatises of Government*, published in 1689, but written a decade earlier. The first Treatise attacked Robert Filmer's *Patriarcha*, which had based the authority of the king in the state on the analogy of the authority of the father in the family, and in the process redefined the latter as well as the former. Marriage was stated to be a mere contractual relationship giving "common interest and property," but not, for example, the power of life and death over a wife. It was argued that the power of the father over his children is merely a utilitarian by-product of his duty to nourish them until they can look after themselves. It is thus only a limited and temporary authority.... In any case parental authority is irrelevant to the authority of a king, to which adults voluntarily submit on condition that he acts for their own good. [*Marriage, Sex, and Family*, p. 164]

far more concrete about the need for adjustment in order to secure continuity of social tradition. The brilliance with which she plots adjustment derives from her utterly clear-eyed perception of the contradictory pressures I have been outlining. She knows, as Burke wants not to know, that in the transition from custom to capital the system of family life among the gentry must give way—indeed is giving way—to the necessities being created by industrial capitalism. In her best fiction Austen tries to give dramatic shape to the adjustments by means of which family bonds, as she values them, might be secured under the developing new conditions. She is especially sensitive to the fact that by the end of the eighteenth century and the beginning of the nineteenth, the lesser gentry who concern her are in a far more exposed situation than they were when Mary Astell wrote in 1730. Cobbett documents the virtual collapse of this class after the Napoleonic wars. Consequently Austen gives proper place to the need to consolidate holdings. But she reverses Astell's emphases to accommodate the imperatives of personal fulfillment. Subservience to family holdings, she acknowledges, would be merely reactionary. To thrive, the system of life of the gentry must embody the contemporary ideal of freedom. Therefore, although Austen chastises Mr. Bennet, she sides with him against the blindly practical Mrs. Bennet. Similarly she insists that Darcy's *estate*, in the full meaning of the word, will be strengthened not by an alliance with the sickly daughter of Lady Catherine but through marriage to Elizabeth. Austen also gives trade its necessary due, endorsing its power by granting it respectability. Finally, Austen has a thorough grasp of the paradox that faces the gentry: that maintenance of status, system, and family has to be negotiated by means of courtship.

Austen stresses in courtship the perils of individual choice. No longer an arrangement between families negotiated by the adults, often without the knowledge of the young couple, marriage is now very clearly the domain of the young. The young of a certain class mingle either in such national marriage markets as Bath or in such smaller local gatherings as county balls. Even when, in her novels, courtship occurs in fairly old-fashioned ways—as, say, between Maria Bertram and Rushworth—the active relationship is unquestionably between the young. Sir Thomas may not be eager to hear his daughter's views or feelings in this matter, but neither does he arrange her wedding. Austen, then, shows us in her novels men and women who, having stepped out of the known stability of family, face in the no-man's-land of courtship the charged combination of possibility and threat. Courtship puts everything at stake, tests the individual in a pressing engagement with the self, with others and finally with one other, and with the society. In *Pride and Prejudice* the Bennet daughters are forced to make their way by means of, at best, a liberating marriage. Against such marriage stands the certainty of a drab, relatively impoverished spinsterhood and the horrors of a barren, emotionally chilling "prudent" marriage. One does not want to damn oneself to life with Mr. Collins, but one worries that marrying Wickham "for love" will be, in Mary Astell's word, Folly. On the other hand, to marry Darcy just for the money, when one thinks of him, as Elizabeth originally does, as arrogantly ungentlemanly, is to save one's body only to lose one's soul.

These dangerous choices mirror the real possibilities of life in the society, not just in the marriages the society makes available but indeed in the generally available choices of social role and vocation. The dangers are precisely the dangers of social mobility at a particular historical juncture. This mobility was both unprecedented—and thus different from our own in that it could not be taken as a matter of course— and forced upon individuals by industrial capitalism. Artisans could become rich; there were dizzying possibilities of wealth, power, career; conditions in the countryside pushed young and old to the cities, but the new cities also drew people to them. One had to choose between the old ways of work or relationship which persisted—say, handloom weaving or certain kinds of trade, farming, or marriage—and new but uncertain or unknown possibilities—factory work, agricultural "improvement," urban life. Although duty and family might direct one's choices, it was clear there were choices to be made, choices that *had* to be made. In some cases one might be able to choose a sure income, a life analogous to marriage with Mr. Collins; or one might choose a risky but glamorous vocation—the equivalent, say, of marriage with Wickham; or one might sell oneself, in the increasingly various ways the society now provided, for great (or small) riches.

Industrial capitalism in this way made choice a condition of life and gave courtship the prominence Austen so brilliantly explicates. Concerned with choice, Austen pays scant attention to the life before and after courtship; especially, she does not follow the newly married couple into their achieved life. As a result her novels express the new ideals of bourgeois ascendance—hopefulness, individual freedom, mobility. The dangers of mobility are noted but they are inevitably overcome. Just as laissez faire ideology, in its ebullience, ignores the disruptive and disastrous aspects of industrial capitalism, so Austen ignores the possibility that the hopefulness of courtship might translate, even for complex characters, into a bitter marriage with Casaubon.

I think there are a number of reasons for Austen's refusal to look beyond courtship. In his 1977 essay, "The Family and the City," Philippe Ariès argues that industrial capitalism divided human activity into two contradictory areas: work and home. At work one is an individual productive unit; but the home, the family, he says, is not a place for individualism.[16] This analysis suggests an explanation for the centrality of courtship in Austen's work and for the shift of attention from courtship to marriage later in the century. Austen wants to affirm the idea of the family—as the literal embodiment of and as the key

16. In *Daedalus*, 106, no. 2 (Spring 1977), 227–35.

symbol of the life of the gentry—yet to urge an adjustment of the older system of allegiances to allow individualism greater prominence. The perseverance of the gentry, she suggests in her novels, is threatened by the flawed and feeble marriages of the older generation: the idea of the family will therefore be redeemed by the wiser arrangements of her heroines and heroes. She contains the contradictory demands of individualism and communal self-restraint in courtship. The novels therefore trace a circle because Austen is satisfied that the traditional family will be bolstered rather than threatened by the individualism set loose in courtship.

An important element of this redemptive process is class reconciliation. Austen argues in her novels that notions of irreconcilable divergence of interest between the lesser gentry and the greater, or between trade and land, are faulty and self-destructive. Darcy's marriage to Elizabeth strengthens them both not simply because they bring to each other valuable personal qualities, but because their marriage creates a saving network of connections between the classes—between the Gardiners and the de Bourghs in particular. The structure of courtship allows Austen to end *Pride and Prejudice* without either rupture or transcendence. This essential quality of plot in that novel, the key feature of its happy ending, amounts to the protection Austen's art affords against life.

This is not altogether a negative quality, for Austen achieves a kind of modernized ritual. Elizabeth Bennet's story is a bourgeois fairy tale; it enacts, in a ritual fashion and by means of a ritual closure, the social aspirations, the resonant fantasies of the middle class. This is the secret power of the structure of courtship as an aesthetic form in the novel. I do not mean to suggest, however, that the happy ending of *Pride and Prejudice* is merely ceremonial or a formulaic evasion of "real life." On the contrary, the novel's ending carries its meaning. Elizabeth expresses the middle-class reader's desire for individual fulfillment through social mobility—expresses the ideological fantasy of the rising class—and contains this desire within the safe bounds of her marriage to Darcy. The reconciliations of Austen's plot neutralize class antagonism in the same way that social divisions are neutralized in, say, "Cinderella."

But by mid-century the division between work and home had widened. The notion that individualism might be a means to invigorate community appeared questionable at best. The separation of classes rather than their reconciliation seemed normative. The optimism of laissez faire was severely qualified by child labor, wage slavery, class conflict; and while trade and land may have walked more easily together, or have become interchangeable, industrial capitalism stood in an apparently unmalleable opposition to them. The demand for love as the basis of marriage, with its implicit enfranchisement of women, was far less easily reconciled with the evident exclusion of women from productive life. Finally, by mid-century the earlier scramble—with its possibilities and dangers—had slowed considerably. The structure of courtship carried an implicit, progressive promise of freedom and fulfillment within a reformed society. When this promise in most respects was negated by social developments, novelists turned to an exploration of marriage, to the ways in which promise translated into actuality. The failed marriages of Austen's older generation now came to be seen for what they were, rather than as flawed examples of a sound and certainly redeemable way of life. The marriages that previously had been summarized in two sentences at the end of the book now increasingly became the main action.

In trying to move beyond the novel-as-structure-of-courtship, such novelists as Charlotte Brontë and Charles Dickens—and then George Eliot and Henry James—faced the need for a new formal structure. This need was met unevenly. Jane Austen's attempt in *Mansfield Park* to move beyond courtship indicates the difficulties of later novelists. Although Austen aims for a broader range of effect in *Mansfield Park* than in *Pride and Prejudice*, she relies nonetheless on a circular plot and a conventional happy ending. But in *Mansfield Park* her happy ending no longer rings true. The characteristic weakness of many novels at mid-century is just this curious falseness of resolution. The reconciliations with which Dickens closes *Hard Times*, for example, are strictly formulaic. Set against Gradgrind's school and Stephen's, Louisa's, and Tom's dehumanization, the novel's final chapter seems a fairy tale in the pejorative sense. The same is true of the endings of *Shirley*, *Mary Barton*, *Dombey and Son*, *Our Mutual Friend*, and any number of other novels. In these works the organic development of form out of content has become problematic, and we can even say that content contradicts form. Stephen and Bounderby, John Barton and Carson, Walter Gay and Dombey represent contradictions that the novels cannot reconcile—and for good reason. *Pride and Prejudice* shows that a convincing reconciliation between, among other things, trade and land could be imagined and plotted. This reconciliation, moreover, offers both Darcy and Elizabeth social freedom. But the reconciliation of worker and owner is unimaginable, given the conditions of the society and the manner in which these contradictory representative individuals are portrayed in the novels. Consequently these novels either opt for one possibility over another, and Portsmouth and London are defeated by Mansfield, or plot an ending that wishes away one of the set of contraries: sometimes through the death of a character, as in *Hard Times* and *Mary Barton;* sometimes through the spiriting away of a character, often to the colonies, as in *Mary Barton* again; and sometimes by a sudden transition to make-believe, as in *Shirley, Dombey and Son*, and *Our Mutual Friend.* The novelist's inability to imagine a true reconciliation within the structure of a circular romantic plot produces in each case an ending that contradicts the implicit meaning of the work.

The circular plot, then, is broken on the issues of sex and class. When the demands of women for fulfillment can no longer be contained by a reconciling marriage, or when the claim to a full life is made not by a middle-class woman but by a working-class man, individualism takes on a dangerous tone. For this reason such novels as *Mansfield Park*, *Shirley*, and *Hard Times* display an unresolvable disharmony; in these novels the circular plot functions not as a ritual closure but as a form of social control.

II

The novelist who creates a social world necessarily engages in a kind of politics, for he or she will necessarily dramatize relations of power, within the family, between the sexes, between classes. In giving life to the social forces of his or her society, the novelist is, moreover, in the extremely powerful position of ordering fictional events. And this ordering is likely to reflect, whether more or less consciously or unconsciously, the attitudes, solutions, structure of feeling common in the novelist's class, race, particular milieu—in short, in the novelist's experience.

One of the original and persistent characterizations of the novel has been that it represents a special version of experience itself or, put another way, a special way of experiencing social reality. "The lowest common denominator of the novel genre," Ian Watt argues in *The Rise of the Novel*, is "formal realism." To show what he means, Watt quotes Lamb's remark that to read Defoe "is like reading evidence in a court of Justice," and Hazlitt's similar remark that Richardson "sets about describing every object and transaction, as if the whole had been given in on evidence by an eye-witness."[17] Watt intends these observations to underline the evidential nature of the novel. But these similes invite additional interpretations. It is interesting that Lamb, Hazlitt, and Watt believe the representation of experience in the eighteenth-century novel to be well described as a record of evidence, in the specifically legal

17. Watt, *Rise of the Novel*, p. 34.

sense. This gives us a clue to one element in fiction that was believed to be—and remains—distinctive, and suggests a connection between what otherwise appear to be disparate activities: fiction and the law. Douglas Hay has recently argued that the law—the institutional complex of crime, trial, and punishment—had in the eighteenth century supplanted religious authority as England's dominant legitimizing ideology.[18] "Turn where you will," writes E. P. Thompson, "the rhetoric of eighteenth century England is saturated by the notion of law."[19] But the notion of law, though technically identifiable as justice, fulfilled centrally the rather different function of social control: "The hegemony of the eighteenth century gentry and aristocracy," as Thompson says, "was expressed, above all . . . in the rituals of the study of the Justices of the Peace, in the quarter sessions, in the pomp of Assizes and in the theater of Tyburn."[20] If law served the role of a legitimizing ideology, then its power in consciousness and its connection with fiction are less surprising. And if in consequence the novel could be seen as "evidence," it seems not inappropriate to ask: Should we see the novelist as a prosecuting attorney, an eyewitness, an informer? Who are the accused? And, conversely, who is the reader?

Lamb's and Hazlitt's similes lead us in two directions—back from the scene of trial to the scene of the crime, or more generally to the world of street and forest, the public arena of the society; and forward from the trial to punishment. This complex of relationships was obviously familiar and imaginatively present for Lamb and Hazlitt as an evocative aspect of the experience of transformation from custom to capital. And it can be seen to have functioned—for them and others—at

18. "Property, Authority, and the Criminal Law," in Douglas Hay et al., *Albion's Fatal Tree: Crime and Society in Eighteenth-Century England* (New York: Pantheon Books, 1975), p. 29.

19. E. P. Thompson, *Whigs and Hunters: The Origin of the Black Act* (New York: Pantheon Books, 1975), p. 263.

20. Ibid., p. 262.

once as a network of ideas, an ideology; as a way of seeing, a structure for the rendering of experience; and as experience itself—in the street, in the courtroom, before the gallows, and in the prisons. Here is one sense of this complex in Dorothy George's standard account of life in eighteenth-century London:

> Throughout the century Londoners lived in a world in which violence, disorder and brutal punishment (though decreasing) were still part of the normal background of life. Newgate, the gallows, the exploits of felons, figured largely in the press and in the current literature of the day. . . . An education in brutality was given in the public spectacles at Tyburn and at the pillory, by the constant floggings through the streets, by the methods of press-gangs and crimps.[21]

This is a very interesting and revealing description. It speaks of "violence, disorder and brutal punishment" as the "normal background of life." But surely they cannot have been "background" either for those who suffered violence or for those who were subjects or perpetrators of brutal punishment. Rather than background, what seems to be described is a particular experience. Hidden in Dorothy George's passage are the class relations definitive of this experience. She writes that "an education in brutality was given" but, in the obscurantism of the passive voice, avoids saying who gave and who received such education. She assumes the violence of felons, which we may grant, but her list of barbarous acts in fact shows mainly a barbarous officialdom. So that one picks up the crucial word "disorder" and wonders just what she means by it. To the criminal "disorder" may have meant the person or activity of the "trading justice" for whom administration of law, as Dorothy George shows, was a business in fees, fines, and bribes; and then "disorder" may have meant, to the criminal, the business of the turnkeys and the bureaucracy of the prisons. But looked at from above, perhaps from where Jeremy

21. M. Dorothy George, *London Life in the Eighteenth Century* (Harmondsworth: Penguin Books, 1966 [first published 1925]), p. 18.

Bentham sat writing up his benevolent schemes, the "disorder" was below. In Dorothy George's account, too, "disorder" shifts easily from fact to fiction: from the gallows to the current literature of the day. Tyburn is both a place of hanging, the occasion and locale of the actual taking of an actual human life, and spectacle. Thompson refers to Tyburn as theater. From our vantage point, as we look back, what takes shape is less disorder than a specific ordering of experience, the creation of image and ideology by various means in the interests of rule. If we remove from Dorothy George's standard history the standard prejudices, the real process of transformation emerges not as the imposition of order on disorder but as a long change from one system to another. The older system appears as disorder if we look back at it without granting it its own value and logic—if we see not the network of relationships but simply violence, brutality, and corruption. Then clearly what happened was the ordering of civil life as a moral positive.

This is certainly Dorothy George's conclusion. The positive historical reaction by the gentry and aristocracy to the violent background of life was, in her words, "improvements in administration and police."[22] These improvements occurred, interestingly, partly under the humane direction and under the urging of the novelist Henry Fielding. As chief magistrate for Westminster (beginning in 1749), George tells us, Fielding "made his office a public place for the administration of justice instead of a justice-shop for trafficking in fines and commitments, and set himself to composing instead of inflaming 'the quarrels of beggars and porters.'"[23] "The administration of justice"—that fine phrase—suggests as the source of order a rationalizing, bureaucratically clean social policy. Education in brutality becomes education in the rule of law or, more specifically, in the *administration* of justice. Disputes are now

22. Ibid., p. 19.
23. Ibid.

to be "composed." That is all very well so far as it goes, which is just short of examination of the justice Fielding administered. "The criminal law," according to Douglas Hay, "was critically important in maintaining obedience and deference, in legitimizing the status quo, in constantly recreating the structure of authority which arose from property and in turn protected its interests."[24] Between 1688 and 1820 capital statutes in England grew from fifty to over two hundred, almost all defining offenses against property.[25] Fielding, committed as he may have been to reform and to the composing of petty quarrels, was perfectly willing to hang men under the proliferating statutes. And if men were hanged for violence, it was usually violence against property. The quarrels of beggars and porters were as nothing compared to the quarrels between handkerchiefs, loaves of bread, trees, pheasants, guineas, and "the mob."

This is not to say that the idea of order being forged out of disorder was not genuinely held or that for many people this idea did not genuinely represent what they believed to be happening in their public relationships and in the life of their communities. Precisely because the law was a legitimizing ideology, its rituals appeared valid. And because the writing of fiction lends itself easily to the view that a novelist imposes order on disorder, and because novelists have as often as not been willing to let this idea stand as valid, the conception of an increasingly orderly social development bears importantly on fiction. But we should not mistake one social policy for order and another for disorder. E. P. Thompson distinguishes three kinds of "order" in the eighteenth century. One was the older system of "manorial and corporate controls," in Thompson's phrase.[26] These controls lost ground because they were effective in maintaining order between ranks and between individuals within a knowable, traditional community rather than

24. Hay et al., *Albion's Fatal Tree*, p. 27.
25. Ibid., p. 25.
26. Thompson, *Whigs and Hunters*, pp. 206–7.

between persons and things of value; but this system nevertheless retained force as an image of a desirable paternalism. The
system of terror characteristic of most of the eighteenth century represented not disorder so much as a calculated discipline intended to shore up and enfranchise the rights of property and of moneyed individuals. But the justification for terror depended on the presupposition of a small community in
which human relationships were relatively intimate. Ritual
punishment was to serve an exemplary function: even in London, a hanging, it was assumed, would be seen by large numbers of people, and so would at the same time be seen to have
its deterrent effect. This structure of feeling, dominant
through the middle of the eighteenth century, in turn gave
way, but gradually and over the span of at least a century, to
an administration of justice enamored of bureaucratic order
and utilitarian rationality, and offended by what increasingly
appeared to be an excess of confusion, violence, and crudity in
public life. The instrument of this finally triumphant notion
of order was the penitentiary, an institution that before the
late eighteenth century was peripheral to the system of criminal justice.[27]

Hazlitt illuminates the nature of the latter development in
an essay on capital punishment he wrote for the *Edinburgh
Review* of July 1821. In his essay Hazlitt quotes from the
testimony of one Mr. Harmer, apparently a prosecuting attorney at the Old Bailey, before the parliamentary Select Committee on Criminal Laws. This committee had, in 1819, issued
a report favoring abolition of some capital statutes. Harmer's
argument is that capital punishment operates far less effectively as a deterrent—if at all—than might other, lesser
punishments. He proposes instead of capital punishment

> a course of discipline totally reversing former habits. *Idleness* is
> one of the prominent characteristics of a professed thief—put
> him to labour:—*Debauchery* is another quality, abstinence is its

27. See Michael Ignatieff, *A Just Measure of Pain: The Penitentiary in the
Industrial Revolution, 1750-1850* (London: Macmillan, 1978), pp. 15-23.

opposite, apply it:—*Dissipated Company* is a thing they indulge in; they ought, therefore, to experience solitude:—they are accustomed to *uncontrolled liberty of action;* I would consequently impose restraint and decorum.[28]

Harmer urges that if his system of discipline were imposed it would be far more effective in curbing crime than capital punishment or the extant prison system. In the past, he says, a convicted thief often asked to be committed to Newgate "because he could there associate with his companions, and have his girl sleep with him, which, some years back, used to be allowed or winked at by the upper turnkeys: but, since the late regulations [thieves no longer ask to go to Newgate] because now they are as much restrained and kept in order in Newgate as in other prisons."[29]

Harmer's intention is clearly to effect a humane reformation, and to substitute the efficacy of improvement for barbarous retribution. Nevertheless, the key words of his account are the final "kept in order." The aim of discipline is to modify behavior toward the approved goal of "order," and order is not here nebulous but spelled out: it means labor, solitude, abstinence, and restraint. Where Harmer got such an idea of order doesn't require comment. It is clear, in any event, why to him the picture of the older Newgate, in which old and young, men and women, mingled and lived in common, more or less at liberty within the walled confines of the prison—it is clear why Harmer saw this picture as abhorrent.[30] It is also clear, I

28. *The Complete Works of William Hazlitt,* ed. P. P. Howe after the edition of A. R. Waller and Arnold Glover (21 vols.; London: J. M. Dent, 1930–34), XIX, 249. Harmer's proposals and way of thinking are not original. Behind him was the thinking of Bentham, Priestley, Wedgwood, Benjamin Rush. And three-quarters of a century earlier Henry Fielding "proposed the construction of a new house of correction for Middlesex. In this institution, prisoners would be roused by a bell and work from 6:00 am until 7:00 pm; their labors would be punctuated by a 'short lecture or exhortation of morality'" (Ignatieff, *Just Measure of Pain,* p. 46).

29. *Complete Works of William Hazlitt,* XIX, 249.

30. Ignatieff writes: "The architecture of the old Newgate, and even of the new Newgate opened in 1770, encouraged the flowering of inmate subcultures. While the design of [the modern, rationalist penitentiary] Penton-

think, why the moral reformation he proposes in the place of death might be more feared by criminals than death. What he advocates is less the liberation of society from unusual punishment or the absolution of the condemned than the imposition of utilitarian regimentation, a regimentation exactly the same as the factory discipline being imposed on the working population as a whole. It is the imposition of one order to replace another. The issue in Newgate as much as in the workplaces is one of control. Would the inmates order the prison or would the jailers? Would the worker control his labor or the capitalist?

The most graphic and powerful expression of these conflicting notions of order is found in a work that doubtless influenced Harmer, Jeremy Bentham's *Panopticon*. Called Bentham's "masterpiece" by Leslie Stephen, it has more recently been judged to be "the zenith point of the bourgeois imagination in its quest for the total control of the working class."[31] Argued for by Bentham mainly as a plan for a model jail—and now known in this way—it was both in its origin and in its conception of far wider application. The idea for the Panopticon was actually that of Bentham's brother Samuel. He created it as an organizational scheme for subduing an unruly work force, the skilled part of which was made up of English craftsmen, which Samuel superintended when he was employed in the 1780s by the Russian prince Potemkin to establish a vast industrial works. Later Samuel applied the principles of the Panopticon to the complex work processes of ship-

---

ville isolated and exposed the inmate before the gaze of authority, Newgate was a dark, damp warren of wards, yards, privies, and staircases nowhere affording authority a clear vantage point for inspection and control" (*Just Measure of Pain*, p. 39).

31. Leslie Stephen, *The English Utilitarians: Jeremy Bentham, James Mill, J. S. Mill* (3 vols.; London: Duckworth, 1900), I, 200; Peter Linebaugh, "The Passage from Workers' Power in the Period of Manufacture: Samuel Bentham, Technological Repression, and the Eighteenth-Century British Shipyards," paper presented to the American Political Science Association, September 1976, p. 7.

building in his role as inspector general of His Majesty's Naval Works at Deptford.³² The implications of the scheme and its imaginative potential, however, were grasped by Jeremy, who gave the Panopticon its detailed shape and its fame. The breadth of Jeremy's conception is clear from the full title he gave the idea in its published form:

> *Panopticon; or the Inspection House: containing the Idea of a new principle of construction applicable to any sort of establishment, in which persons of any description are to be kept under inspection, and in particular to penitentiary-houses, prisons, houses of industry, work-houses, poor-houses, manufactories, hospitals, and schools: with a plan of management adapted to the principle: in a series of letters written in the year 1787, from Crecheff in White Russia, to a friend in England.*

"Persons of any description . . . under inspection": prisons, manufactories, schools—they are the same to Bentham. For him, that is, the Panopticon scheme is applicable to the key institutions of order under industrial capitalism.

> *Morals reformed—health preserved—industry invigorated—instruction diffused—public burthens lightened—Economy seated, as it were, upon a rock—the gordian knot of the Poor Laws not cut, but untied—all by a single idea in Architecture!*³³

These are the words that open Bentham's account. The breadth of his intention, as well as its unabashed aim of social control, is clear. The architectural idea is indeed ingeniously simple and, in its imagery and symmetry, a startlingly graphic expression of economic individualism. The Benthams proposed to build institutions on the plan, roughly, of a bicycle wheel and its spokes. At the center of this circular building would stand an "inspector"; from his privileged vantage point he would be able to watch all of the "cells" or seats or benches or machines of those enclosed or imprisoned in the institution,

---

32. See Linebaugh, "Passage from Workers' Power."

33. *The Works of Jeremy Bentham*, published under the superintendence of his executor John Bowring (12 vols.; New York: Russell & Russell, 1962 [1838–43]), IV, 39.

for the cells would be distributed along the periphery of the wheel, the walls of each cell following, as it were, the lines of the many spokes. Initially, in his model for a penitentiary, Bentham took this extreme notion to its logical conclusion and proposed one small cell per prisoner; similarly he proposed, for schools, a model in which each student's desk and bed would be walled off from those of each other student. The Panopticon achieves a demoniac individualism: each inmate is totally separated from each other inmate, and all he or she can see is the centrally placed "inspector"; but the inspector, at a glance, can at all times view the actions of all the inmates. "The essence of [the plan] consists," Bentham writes, "in the *centrality* of the inspector's situation, combined with the well-known and most effectual contrivances for '*seeing without being seen.*'" This is the plan's ingenious essence because, Bentham says, "it is obvious, in all these instances [i.e., prisons, factories, schools], that the more constantly the persons to be inspected are under the eyes of the persons who should inspect them, the more perfectly will the purpose of the establishment have been attained. Ideal perfection . . . would require that each person should actually be in that predicament during every instant of time. This being impossible, the next thing to be wished for is, that . . . he should *conceive* himself to be so." This plan applies to *all* institutions, including schools. There "all play, all chattering—in short, all distraction of every kind, is effectually banished by the central and covered situation of the master, seconded by partitions or screens between the scholars, slight as you please."[34]

Michel Foucault's ingenious exploration of punishment in his *Surveiller et punir*[35] suggests a bridge between Bentham's "simple idea" and the novel during the Industrial Revolution. Foucault argues that the prison, like the factory, aims through

34. Ibid., pp. 44, 40, 63; Bentham's italics.
35. Michel Foucault, *Surveiller et punir: Naissance de la prison* (Paris: Gallimard, 1975).

coercion and regimentation to achieve an acquiescent docility. Organized around the key principles of centralization and observation—or inspection—the prison, in isolating prisoners and subjecting them to observation, at once makes them individuals—to themselves and to their jailers—and paradoxically reduces them to "cases." Extending social control by means of a generalized surveillance, the prison permits a particular kind of social study: the study of the individual. The change from the disorder of a communal Newgate to the order of the Panopticon yields, then, a kind of individuated knowledge especially appropriate to its age.

Jonathan Arac has pointed to one passage in the English novel which illuminates this point: "Oh for a good spirit who would take the housetops off, with a more potent and benignant hand than the lame demon in the tale, and show a Christian people what dark shapes issue from amidst their homes, to swell the retinue of the Destroying Angel as he moves forth among them" (*Dombey and Son*, chap. 47).[36] This is one passage, a critical one, but one thinks of many others, including, to choose a continental example, Balzac's description of Mme Vauquer's boardinghouse as a prison composed of so many cells. If you take the housetops off, as the novelist may and Dickens aims to, you reproduce Bentham's Panopticon as an image and as a complex of relationships. The picture drawn is, I think, especially striking, the honeycomb pattern in which each individual is walled in within his own living cell. Dickens's expressed aim is benevolent: if one could see, one would understand; and understanding, as he goes on to argue in his charged paragraph, would break down the walls and reestablish the awareness that we are "creatures of one common

36. My understanding of Foucault, the Panopticon, and their relation to Dickens depends on Jonathan Arac's "Michel Foucault's *Surveiller et punir: The Place of the Criminal*," presented at the Northeast Victorian Studies Association Conference on Victorian Crime and Punishment, Boston College, April 15–17, 1977. Other papers at the conference to which I am indebted are Robert B. MacKay's "The Architecture of Prisons" and W. Robert Carr's "The Ironic Humanity of Bentham's Panopticon."

origin . . . tending to one common end." Such understanding would "make the world a better place." But his aim is less striking than the correspondence between his vision and Bentham's: in each the central point is observation, the ability to see without being seen; in each the sense of individuation occurs by means of distance; in each the fixed poles of meaning are inspector and inspected; in each the image of order gets expressed in terms of cells that contrast with the chaos and disorder of people in the streets, in groups and classes. Knowledge of self and of society comes out of a particular kind of inspection.

Lamb and Hazlitt suggest the novel resembles evidence, perhaps of an eyewitness, in a court of law. But Defoe's and Richardson's novels suggest less the sense of eyewitness than that of autobiography. Moll Flanders tells her own story— perhaps in court, or a kind of court (she asks forgiveness at the close), but in her own voice. If she is under observation, the observer is well hidden: the author hides within the character, disclaims the "fiction," and wants to achieve immediacy, colloquial vividness, and a train of compelled individual action, under pressure, from moment to moment. Nor does one sense in Defoe or Richardson that the events their characters narrate present themselves as disorder, as a chaos to be partitioned and subdued. Rather, in *Moll Flanders* and *Clarissa*, the unraveling of the individual experience serves as an adequate, appropriate structure for plot and meaning. In these novels the characters are not under inspection but, on the contrary, speak for themselves. It is rather Tom Jones who is observed; he is the obvious and outstanding exception. But the rising voices and forms are of those usually outside polite literature and outside polite society, and they speak of their own lives in forms that suit them. The selectivity that governs *Moll Flanders* is the ordinary selectivity we expect in autobiography: I tell you this because it happened to me; this is *my* story, listen to *me*. Here the individual looks out at society, to find himself or herself and to uncover social meaning.

This way to knowledge, although I think it finds its great expression in the nineteenth century in *Jane Eyre*, and continues as the structural form of self-expression by various "outsiders" from Samuel Bamford to the novelist Jack Common, yet did not reflect the complexity of social movement as clearly or of course as schematically as what I have already spoken of as the structure of courtship. One element that gives the structure of courtship its classic, ritual dimension is the tense balance of attention to individual and society, to complaint and restraint, to self-fulfillment and duty. If in *Pride and Prejudice* Austen looks on, perhaps as an eyewitness, she also takes care not to set in view, except by indirection and suggestion, the disruptive social elements that might preclude balance and reconciliation. *Pride and Prejudice* asserts a unitary culture. If the structure of courtship expressly aims to dramatize danger and dangerous choice, it is finally also an affirming structure. Its end is change without threat to stability. But in such novels as *Mansfield Park*, *Shirley*, *Mary Barton*, *Dombey and Son*, and *Hard Times* the need to establish order out of more or less distantly observed disorder becomes far more pressing. Precisely what we don't see in *Pride and Prejudice* now comes under inspection.

At Mansfield, no sounds of contention, no raised voice, no abrupt bursts, no tread of violence was ever heard. . . . [*Mansfield Park*, III, chap. 8]

It was not the tread of two, nor of a dozen, nor of a score of men: it was the tread of hundreds. [*Shirley*, II, chap. 19]

The actions of the uneducated seem to me typified in those of Frankenstein, that monster of many human qualities, ungifted with a soul, a knowledge of the difference between good and evil.

The people rise up to life; they irritate us, they terrify us, and we become their enemies. [*Mary Barton*, chap. 15]

Then was it not the sacred duty of the men of Coketown, with forefathers before them, an admiring world in company with them, and a posterity to come after them, to hurl out traitors. . . ? The winds of heaven answered, Yes; and bore

Yes, east, west, north, and south. And consequently three
cheers for the United Aggregate Tribunal!

                    . . .

   Thus easily did Stephen Blackpool fall into the loneliest of
lives, the life of solitude among a familiar crowd. [*Hard
Times*, bk. 2, chap. 4]

A certain narrative distance, Elizabeth Gaskell's "we," becomes characteristic when the novel comes in touch with masses, aggregates, the people, the crowd. The attributes of this
crowd are uniformly those Austen singles out to define
Portsmouth: contention, raised voices, abrupt outbursts, the
tread of violence. Here is Dorothy George's background of
life, assessed much in her terms, but with its own political
edge. When, in the novels I have noted, George's background
becomes foreground, this transposition is taken to indicate the
appearance *within* even the narrow family circle of a troubling
and threatening disorder. This disorder, much like the disorder Austen finds repellent in *Mansfield Park*, makes
knowledge—of the self, of society, of moral value—at best
difficult and perhaps impossible. Austen judges that such a
person as Fanny, sensitive to the nuances of elegance and
moral propriety, cannot live at Portsmouth: such a condition,
Austen argues, would kill her. When the violent background
of life envelops the individual, and rather than a distanced
chaos becomes the daily "necessity" out of which one must
make one's life, certain ways of living and certain values
become—Austen says—unattainable. In *Mansfield Park*, then,
as in the novels that follow, the experienced threat is to the
English novel's essential values: the values of personal well-
being and moral and aesthetic personal relations. The threat is
very serious indeed. The crisis comes about, too, because
what, at least in Austen, once ensured the viability of these
values—the societal network—now is itself seen as the source
of threat, disruption, and instability.

   But although *Mansfield Park* shows how and why the threat
of disorder is serious, it is of course an uncharacteristic book

insofar as it only implies a class dimension to disorder. But in *Shirley*, Brontë talks of the tread of hundreds; in *Mary Barton*, Gaskell judges "the uneducated" and "the people"; in *Hard Times*, Dickens opposes Stephen to an "Aggregate" and a "crowd." The indirection and suggestion of *Mansfield Park*, permitted by Austen's isolation in a landed enclave, give way to the confrontations of the industrial north and of London: background becomes foreground. The social and aesthetic exemplum of the landed estate and its courtships is itself now cast in the background of life as the Industrial Revolution raises the fact of class.

Walter Allen argues that what the English novel is about is class.[37] But because on the whole novels depict middle-class perceptions, and during the Industrial Revolution middle-class perceptions of the working class, what is registered on the whole is a sense of shock. The question of class, in other words, is not a question of content in itself, but of the total impact of class—as a disturbance—on the writer's structure of feeling. The distinction between form and content is hard to maintain in the light of class; and once the turbulence of industrial relations, with its Aggregates, becomes the main given, the shock felt by the writer is registered in the whole of his or her work—in diction, structure, plot, characterization.

Once the writer sets out to create a novel in which masses occupy the foreground, he or she faces the problem of how masses can be "realized" in a novel. The tradition of the English novel during the period of industrialization was not, in this respect, helpful. The whole thrust of the English novel, with its care for personal relations, had been—and has continued to be—toward expression of an individual life. I have tried to show how this emphasis produced novels of great power and authenticity, such as *Jane Eyre*. Even when a novel subsumes the individual within what was considered a nurturing social network, as does *Pride and Prejudice*, the stress on

37. Walter Allen, *The English Novel* (London: Phoenix House, 1954).

personal relations and moral crisis within personal relations
obviously remain central. How then could a writer talk about
masses? The structure of courtship, one would have thought,
just would not do. Yet, remarkably, it persisted—even in
Mary Barton, even in *Hard Times*, even in *Dombey and Son*. But
more important than the continuation of this structure as a
kind of relic was the primacy of individuation as a way of
seeing and of gaining knowledge about individual and social
life. The novelists I am speaking of proceed precisely as
Bentham does: the disorder of the mass, its unknowableness,
is broken down by means of various kinds of partitioning. In
order to study the working class the novelist isolates one or
two individuals, and then studies this encapsulated person in
his or her separateness. I think this partitioning is clearly a
protective means to cope with the shock of a violent mass. But,
too, it expresses, in Bentham as in Brontë, Gaskell, and Dickens, the unquestioned ideological maxim that value resides in
individuation. The individual is free, though by implication
usually only when the individual, by virtue of his or her class,
at the same time exemplifies order. The crowd, the working-
class mass, breeds—*is*—disorder. The social individual is
created in the novels as in the Panopticon by isolation, separation, severance from his or her social base, confinement. Such
partitioning and restriction, paradoxically, enable the creation
in social life of the values associated with the individual: quiet,
cleanliness, propriety, personal harmony, and the "capacity"
for personal relations—in short, "order."

Some of the costs and benefits of such individuation can be
illustrated by a comparison of Fanny Price and Jane Eyre. The
initial situations in which we meet Fanny and Jane are remarkably similar. We find them as young girls, more or less as
orphans, each struggling to maintain herself in a hostile country house of wealthy relatives. Order and disorder are central
themes in each novel. It appears, initially, that each girl is
herself a cause of disorder, and that this disorder derives
somehow from her inferior social origin. As the books de-

velop, however, we come to see a more complex situation: the
disorder turns out to be in the country houses themselves, in
Mrs. Reed and her children and in Sir Thomas and his. Each
novel strives to establish true grounds for personal and social
order. But whereas Brontë gives Jane her own voice and gives
us Jane's experience through Jane's eyes, Austen creates
Fanny from a distance: she is precisely observed. And whereas
Fanny, even in the early sections of *Mansfield Park*, is the
moral center of the novel, order derives from the conventions
and standards of Mansfield itself, as a social system, as a
house, as a symbol. The occupants of Mansfield have failed it;
Fanny redeems it by understanding the place of her confinement better than they do. Enclosed, she finds her identity in
enclosure. In contrast, Jane strikes out against the conventions
that try to establish her identity by enclosing it. Jane lives in
the vital imaginative turbulence of Bewick's pictures and of
her emotional needs. Her whole impulse is organic: to flower,
to burst into bloom, to express her inner self. Therefore in
place after place Jane fights to get out of the rooms assigned to
her, the cells that are intended to differentiate and defuse her
personal force by a restrictive social placement. The novel
affirms Jane's resistance, argues that conventionality is not
morality. But Fanny finds in her small unheated room, her
ascetic cell, stability and meaning. In doing so she reflects the
essential direction of *Mansfield Park*, its intention to discover
individuality by means of restraint and enclosure. One thinks,
for example, of the sexually charged scenes at Sotherton,
which so carefully place value and danger—the former within
the walls and gates of the estate, the latter beyond the pale in
Sotherton's "wilderness."

Mansfield dramatizes, then, the paradox of confinement.
Confinement enables individuation. Confinement means an
elegant individual privacy and is opposed to the unruly, indec-
orous scramble of Portsmouth. But—paradoxically—the gain
of these bourgeois values comes at a price, the price of confinement. This confinement is at once literal and, more impor-

tant, emotional. We may say positively, with Austen, that *Mansfield Park* demonstrates the impossibility of a social existence that is not socially entangled, that the individual is impossible—and thus necessarily enslaved—without society. But this view affirms a particular, wealthy social life and a limited, decorous individualism. The restraint Austen affirms looks to Jane Eyre like imprisonment: it amounts to a repression of the self's deeper energies. When Miss Temple leaves Lowood and when Jane has become accustomed to the placid routine at Thornfield before Rochester's arrival, she stands in each place at a window and longs for freedom, for a freedom beyond the visible horizon. She wants to get out. She wants to have done with isolation, to mingle with others, to experience the busy life of the city crowd. The literal freedom of open country and busy life state the emotional freedom she longs for.

Upon reading *Pride and Prejudice*, Brontë wrote what better applies to *Mansfield Park*. She found in the novel "a carefully-fenced, highly-cultivated garden, with neat borders and delicate flowers; but no glance of a bright, vivid physiognomy, no open country, no fresh air, no blue hill, no bonny beck. I should hardly like to live with her ladies and gentlemen, in their elegant but confined houses."[38]

Yet the tread of hundreds in *Shirley* complicates and qualifies Brontë's criticism of Austen. She may still be wary of ladies and gentlemen and of elegant confinement, but she can find nothing more positive in the life of the crowd or in the concept of social class. To see people as representative of their class is repulsive to her: she would have us see them only as individuals. The crowd is threatening and dangerous, so threatening and dangerous that she dare not give it its own voice, even in the circumscribed form of a fully realized individual leader. The immediacy of *Jane Eyre* is replaced by a

38. Letter to G. H. Lewes, quoted in Elizabeth Cleghorn Gaskell, *Life of Charlotte Brontë* (London: J. M. Dent, 1958), p. 240.

very careful, even a nervous authorial distance. Everything is
at arm's length. That Frankenstein monster the people, ignor-
ant of good and evil, unable to know itself and thus a barrier to
all knowledge, must be subject to the stern, even dictatorial
control of the gentry and the manufacturers and of an equally
repressive narrative structure.

Brontë's friend Elizabeth Gaskell manages better in *Mary
Barton*. The startling thing about this novel is the extent of its
respect for the integrity and autonomy of John Barton. Gaskell's book consequently records one especially troubling contradiction that necessarily follows when a creature of disorder
is given voice in the novel. This is, bluntly, the contradiction
between the class allegiances of author and character. In *Mansfield Park* the author's stance as observer is sanctioned by the
character's identification with the values of the confining social and aesthetic structure. A creature of her creator and of
Mansfield, Fanny betrays her origins and embraces as liberating her social and—if I may put it this way—her aesthetic
confinement. In *Jane Eyre* confinement appears as a denial of
liberty rather than as a liberating individuation. It is as if
Fanny had turned against Mansfield and, later in life, written
an outraged account of her elegant incarceration. If *Jane Eyre*
in this way overturns *Mansfield Park*, *Mary Barton* similarly
overturns *Shirley*. In *Mary Barton* the silenced crowd speaks in
the voice of John Barton.

But only to a point, the point at which he threatens to get
out of control. Although Gaskell hedges Barton round with
authorial comment and overt interference—the book does *not*
take the form of autobiography—nonetheless she lets him
speak his mind and lets events take their course. Having
granted Barton his autonomy, Gaskell is drawn inexorably to
narrate an irreconcilable conflict between classes; moreover,
because Barton can be himself in the novel's early sections,
Gaskell is pushed to justify his actions and beliefs at the expense of those of her own class. It is at this point, when Barton
threatens as a character to get out of the control of his author,

that she silences him. Once he murders Harry Carson, Barton disappears from the novel; we never see him again. The character who returns to the stage of the novel with Barton's name is not John Barton but a cardboard imposter: the Barton who returns, drained and repentant, is wholly Gaskell's puppet and no longer a voice with its own integrity. Having begun the novel as an individual, Barton becomes by the end a case.

But the Barton who speaks briefly in his own voice damages the novel-as-structure-of-courtship beyond repair. His dramatized experience denies the unitary nature of the society. The possibilities of reconciliation in Austen's books depended, as I have said, on class reconciliation; this reconciliation was possible only insofar as the society was seen as a single cultural system. Mr. Bennet and Darcy live very much in the same world. If Austen may be said to possess a comprehensive vision—that vision which Leavis denies Dickens except in *Hard Times*[39]—she achieves it because she draws a whole world on a very small piece of ivory. But Barton shows that in Manchester there are at least two classes, and that those two classes live two wholly distinct ways of life, and that at most points the two ways of life contradict each other. Gaskell strives to assert unity and attain comprehensiveness even after this thorough demonstration, through Barton, that in Manchester there exist two nations. She does so, I would argue, to maintain the middle class's confidence in the middle class, or specifically her own allegiance to her own way of life. Of course I can't prove this to be so. What is beyond speculation, however, is the drastic reworking that the second half of the novel requires, the violence she must use to bring Mary Barton forward. The romance between Mary and Jem comes wholly from the novel-as-structure-of-courtship. It is not a comprehensive vision, and it is barely integrated with the action John Barton initiates. That is to say that Gaskell falls back on a strictly conventional plot. The word "convention" means

39. Or which Leavis denied him until publication of *Dickens the Novelist*.

here something significantly different from what it means
when it is applied to Austen. In Austen's *Pride and Prejudice*
the conventions express the novel's meaning. In Gaskell they
are an imposition, a form of social control and artistic despera-
tion. We are a good way, in *Mary Barton*, toward the meaning
of "convention" in such sentences as "Dickens's happy endings
are just conventional." This sentence is intended to mean that
the sophisticated reader understands the real point of a Dickens novel to be made along the way, in the body of the novel,
in the manner of its observations, in the loosed struggle and
emotion rather than in the plot or the "outcome." The "conventions" are here recognized as merely traditional, dead:
what is new and vital in Dickens goes on elsewhere. My own
view is that you cannot so easily dismiss Dickens's plots or
endings. They too are integral to his structure of feeling. The
disjunction between the ending of *Hard Times* and its action
seems to me a sign of a failed comprehensiveness. This failure
to be comprehensive may not, in itself, be a bad thing; it may,
for example, merely attest to the disunity of the society. But it
is nonetheless a fact. It is a fact that is especially unsettling
because, of the English novelists of the Industrial Revolution,
Dickens pays greatest attention to the crowd.

III

As we stand and look back at a Dickens novel the general
movement we remember—the decisive movement—is a hurrying seemingly random passing of men and women, each heard
in some fixed phrase, seen in some fixed expression: a way of
seeing men and women that belongs to the street. There is at
first an absence of ordinary connection and development.
These men and women do not so much relate as pass each
other and then sometimes collide. . . . But then as the action
develops, unknown and unacknowledged relationships, profound and decisive connections, definite and committing recognitions and avowals are as it were forced into consciousness. . . .

This creation of consciousness—of recognitions and

relationships—seems to me indeed to be the purpose of Dickens' developed fiction.[40]

This is Raymond Williams. Immediately following this passage Williams quotes the sentences from the forty-seventh chapter of *Dombey and Son* I have already noted above ("Oh for a good spirit who would take the housetops off"), and remarks: "That potent and benignant hand, which takes off the housetops... ; which clears the air so that people can see and acknowledge each other... : that is the hand of the novelist; it is Dickens seeing himself."[41] In this way Williams makes his "case" (his word) for Dickens. He argues that Dickens writes "a new kind of novel" uniquely expressive of "a new kind of reality"—"the reality of a new kind of city."[42] This new urban reality, as Williams sees it in Dickens's work, is captured in the apparent contradictions of the street scene: on the one hand a hurrying atomized mass, often obscured in a blindingly polluted literal and figurative atmosphere, apparently inhuman, the human "relation" radically disturbed; on the other, the "decisive connections" made clear by the benevolent intervention of the artist. If we judge Dickens as being not Jane Austen and not George Eliot—in other words, Williams says, if we judge him in the terms of a different kind of novel—we miss his originality and importance; we miss the experience of "consciousness" which it is his "purpose" to create.

Williams makes an argument for Dickens which suggests a transformation in the novel—and in the society—between the initial years of the Industrial Revolution and that point at roughly the mid-nineteenth century when we can say that England had become an industrial society. He attempts an

40. Raymond Williams, *The English Novel from Dickens to Lawrence* (Frogmore, St. Albans, Herts.: Paladin, 1974), p. 29.
    41. Ibid., pp. 29–30.
    42. Ibid., p. 28. F. S. Schwarzbach, *Dickens and the City* (London: Athlone Press, 1979), writes: "Dickens is virtually the only English writer of any stature to engage in a sustained effort to write about the city during the first two thirds of the nineteenth century" (p. 3).

answer to the question by Walter Houghton with which I began this chapter. Because his answer seems to me quite persuasive in general, and especially persuasive as it pertains to Dickens, and because I have some reservations about his answer as it pertains to Dickens, I would like to move to a close by pursuing what I believe are the strengths and weaknesses of Williams's case.

Williams's essay on Dickens should be read side by side with Walter Benjamin's essay on Baudelaire. The two essays reinforce one another, but are illuminatingly different in their approach and scope. Benjamin quotes the following from Baudelaire:

> Who among us has not dreamt, in his ambitious days, of the miracle of a poetic prose? It would have to be musical without rhythm and rhyme, supple and resistant enough to adapt itself to the lyrical stirrings of the soul, the wave motions of dreaming, the shocks of consciousness. This ideal . . . will grip especially those who are at home in the giant cities and the web of their numberless interconnecting relationships;

and comments:

> This passage suggests two insights. For one thing, it tells us about the close connection in Baudelaire between the figure of shock and contact with the metropolitan masses. For another, it tells us what is really meant by these masses. They do not stand for classes or any sort of collective; rather they are nothing but the amorphous crowd of passers-by, the people in the street.[43]

Benjamin argues that the formative connection in Baudelaire's poetry is the connection to the urban crowd. He describes a relationship then very much like the one Williams describes. It is not hard to see in Dickens's work the ambitious dream of a poetic prose. But Benjamin is especially suggestive because, in explaining the desire for such a prose, he differentiates be-

43. Walter Benjamin, *Illuminations*, ed. with an introduction by Hannah Arendt (New York: Schocken, 1969). References in the summary that follows are from "On Some Motifs in Baudelaire," pp. 154–94 *passim*.

tween preindustrial and industrial consciousness. Briefly his analysis is this:

Looking for "clues" to the nature of "experience" under "present-day conditions," Benjamin first turns to Bergson, from whom he concludes that experience is "a matter of tradition. . . . It is less the product of fact firmly anchored in memory than of a convergence in memory of accumulated and frequently unconscious data." To uncover the nature of these data, Benjamin next turns to Proust, and finds in Proust a distinction between voluntary and involuntary memory. Voluntary memory is what is set in motion when Proust tastes his madeleine—a memory, in other words, which leaves no traces of the past, which we don't know we possess, but which lives richly in unconscious associations. Involuntary memory, on the other hand, "bears the marks of the situation which gave rise to it; it is part of the inventory of the individual who is isolated in many ways." Insofar as the individual is aware of a connection between a past situation and a memory, this awareness connects him with a collective experience, as for example in the way that rituals give "handles of memory" to a person's life.

Benjamin now turns to Freud (the Freud of *Beyond the Pleasure Principle*) to make the connection between memory and consciousness. "Consciousness," Benjamin quotes Freud as saying, "comes into being at the site of a memory trace." Freud continues: "It would be the special characteristic of consciousness that, unlike what happens in all other psychical systems, the excitatory process does not leave behind a permanent change in its elements"; in other words, that "becoming conscious and leaving behind a memory trace are processes incompatible with each other within one and the same system." Indeed, Freud suggests, memory fragments are "often most powerful and most enduring when the incident which left them behind was one that never entered consciousness." Freud maintains, Benjamin says, that consciousness receives no memory traces whatever, and that its prime function, in-

stead, is protection against stimuli. He quotes Freud again:
"For a living organism, protection from stimuli is an almost
more important function than the reception of stimuli; the
protective shield is equipped with its own store of energy, and
must above all strive to preserve the special forms of conversion of energy operating in it against the effects of the exces-
sive energies at work in the external world, effects which tend
towards an equalization of potential and hence towards destruction." The point Benjamin wishes to make here is that the
threat to the organism against which consciousness is alert is
the threat from shocks. The function of consciousness is to
parry shocks. If, Benjamin says, a shock "were incorporated
directly in the registry of conscious memory, it would sterilize
this incident for poetic experience." It would do so because
poetic experience depends on the unconscious associations one
has about incidents and objects, associations of which there is
no conscious trace. Having mapped out this complex account
of consciousness, Benjamin now brings it to a climactic point:
"The question suggests itself," he writes, "how lyric poetry
can have as its basis an experience for which the shock experience has become the norm."

The preindustrial consciousness was relatively shockfree,
and experience—by which Benjamin means the traceless mass
of unconscious associations—maintained its richness in the
personal and societal life, and was available to art. The secret
of art came from its "aura," the cluster of unconscious associations around an object of perception. This aura was exploited
in ritual, and in the ritual nature of art.

But under industrial capitalism conditions of life changed to
make the shock experience the norm. For Baudelaire, Benjamin says, the shock experience was connected with the crowd.
The nature of this crowd, for Baudelaire as for most
nineteenth-century writers, was at best contradictory. "Fear,
revulsion, and horror," Benjamin says, "were the emotions
which the big-city crowd aroused in those who first observed
it." This was so because of the apparent inhumanity of the

crowd, its atomizing quality. As Williams writes, "These men and women do not so much relate as pass each other. . . ." But Williams adds: "and then sometimes collide." Here is the second element, the sense of shock. What is repulsive in this experience of shock is its mechanical nature. Benjamin brilliantly demonstrates the generalized "training" in navigation among shocks that occurs in the industrial epoch. He links the invention of the match, the movement of an assembly line or mechanized work process, riding Dodgem cars at a fair, crossing a street in traffic to underline the pervasive subjection of the individual to discontinuous, shocking, automaton-like "experience." At the heart of this experience is that of collision, in its various forms, and the connection among these forms of collision: "The shock experience which the passer-by in the crowd has," Benjamin says, "corresponds to what the worker 'experiences' at his machine."

The consequence of this pervasive perception of shocks is a disintegration of experience, that is, of the body of unconscious association. Aiming to understand a modern artist by first coming to grips with "the special functioning of psychic mechanisms under present-day conditions," Benjamin arrives at the conclusion that present-day conditions have so accelerated the demands on psychic energy to ward off shock as to deplete the bank of unconscious memory. The effort to recoup this loss is recorded, Benjamin believes, in the work of Proust and in some of *Fleurs du mal;* this is the record of *correspondances.* "The important thing is," Benjamin says, "that the *correspondances* record a concept of experience which includes ritual elements. Only by appropriating these elements was Baudelaire able to fathom the full meaning of the breakdown which he, a modern man, was witnessing." "What Baudelaire meant by *correspondances* may be described as an experience which seeks to establish itself in crisis-proof form. This is possible only within the realm of ritual. If it transcends this realm, it presents itself as the beautiful. In the beautiful the ritual value of art appears." The *correspondances,* then, aim to

establish a link with an earlier form of consciousness in which
experience could be expressed as the aura of art. "The *correspondances* are the data of remembrance—not historical remembrance, but data of prehistory. What makes festive days
great and significant is the encounter with an earlier life.
Baudelaire recorded this in a sonnet entitled 'La vie an-
térieure.'" But it is precisely this previous consciousness that
is no longer retrievable. The "beautiful" and ritual are a lost
past; the present is the domain of the street, the crowd, and
the factory. This is at once destructive and liberating. For
Benjamin the full recognition of this new reality accounts for
Baudelaire's greatness: "He indicated the price for which the
sensation of the modern age may be had: the disintegration of
the aura in the experience of shock."

If we look back on the novels I have discussed with Benjamin's and Williams's analyses in mind, a pattern of dialectical
movement emerges. On the one hand there is a defensive
reaction, an effort on the part of the novel (if we can speak of it
for the moment as a corporate abstraction) to protect itself
from shock and maintain the ritual circle. On the other hand
there is the expression of new consciousness. The positive
expression of life under new conditions, with its affirmation of
new possibilities that are seen as genuinely liberating, and the
resistance to new conditions are closely related, sometimes
part of the same response. In *Pride and Prejudice* positive expression and resistance manage a coherence that give the novel
the dimensions of ritual. The exuberance of this novel is the
sign of an energy capable of cushioning the shocks of consciousness. Perhaps we can say that the conflicts of *Pride and
Prejudice* do not rupture the novel because they occur in this
cushioned form. The potentially violent struggle of the individual against his or her family, of child against father, or the
pull of trade against land, remain—in their volatile aspects—
buried within the hidden world of the novel's emotions. Each
of the novel's thematic facts—marriage, the family, money,
class—is felt powerfully precisely because its true weight de-

rives from the realm of assumed association, only more or less conscious, like Elizabeth's unconscious attraction to Darcy in the first half of the novel. The aura of the work of art, in Benjamin's terms, has not here so much disintegrated as become recharged by the connection to the mythology of the new (or emerging) industrial society. The divisive directness of Lady Catherine is rejected in favor of the subtle rapprochement between Darcy and the Gardiners. Perhaps this sense of aura is the achievement of Austen's celebrated irony. Experience and tradition are shown in the novel in an enabling interchange.

But when in *Mansfield Park* Austen actively invokes memory, what she calls into play is merely an idea of the past. Tradition is now a kind of fetish intended to reproduce value in the face of a number of disruptive shocks—those represented by London and the Crawfords, by Portsmouth, and by the hugely threatening financial crisis in Antigua. The critical point is not in the nature of these shocks, I think, but in the narrative method with which Austen meets them. The novel follows a method radically different from that of *Pride and Prejudice*. Its characteristics are the use of narrative as a means of social control and the selective invocation of memory. The novel's doomed purpose is revitalization through repression. Austen attempts to activate tradition so that she may reassert as viable a clearly disintegrating experience—experience in the usual sense, but even more so in Benjamin's sense. For the crisis of paternalism in the novel occurs precisely because the potency of ritual has suffered breakdown under the impact of a wholesale secular apostasy. The scenes at Sotherton and the scenes of domestic acting dramatize the violation of taboo: that is why they are so surprisingly charged despite our inability exactly to pinpoint the source of their emotion. And that, too, is why the novel *is* about ordination, and why Edmund will be a minister.

But once broken, the ritual circle cannot be put back together into its original form, and certainly not by means of force. It is humanly valuable that Sir Thomas is torn from his ceremonial throne, but once he is a man like the rest of us, he loses his ritual immunity. Emptied of its experience—that is, of its cluster of legitimizing associations—Mansfield becomes a very fallible human house, and we cannot see that anything but wealth separates it from the Price household in Portsmouth. The elevation of Fanny as inheritor of Mansfield's experience, its tradition as a system of value, consequently falls far short of a satisfying closure. Once Mansfield has lost the aura of its original dominance, how can we be asked to accept its dominance without any adjustment of terms? Yet that is just what Austen demands of us. Having exposed Mansfield, she nonetheless insists we accept in Fanny and Edmund's marriage the revitalization of Mansfield's value. But can we really be expected to see Fanny and Edmund as patriarchs? Surely Kingsley Amis is right, and what we think instead is that under no circumstances would we have Fanny and Edmund to dinner.[44]

After Austen no English novelist could claim to portray a unitary culture. The positive account of individualism occurred rather in the form of the personal voice Jane Eyre raised against her society. Rather than being bent on parrying the shocks of consciousness so as to persevere, *Jane Eyre* is a vehicle of the driving social and psychic forces that come from within and from below. What Austen sees as disintegration Brontë sees as liberation. The novel insists on a human equality and a human scale; it assaults the ritual mystifications that empowered the country house, the ministry, the romantic male. For this reason one of the fascinating dramas of the novel is its vital but veiled conflict between liberation and repression, morality and conventionality, class and class. Brontë at once gives her desires voice and fears them, assents to her heroine's psychic needs and reins them in. In each

44. Kingsley Amis, "What Became of Jane Austen?," *Spectator*, 199 (1957), 339–40.

section of the novel a dialectical struggle occurs marking the stages of Jane's maturation. In this way we move from Gateshead, where the contradictions in Jane's life explode for the first time, to Lowood, Thornfield, Moor House, and finally Ferndean. It is this movement of growth by means of the synthesis of opposites that defines *Jane Eyre*'s great formal achievement, its leap beyond the novel-as-structure-of-courtship. Moreover, just as the Industrial Revolution was a triumph of the human ability to shape the world, so Jane demonstrates the individual's ability actively to construct her own life. Rather than disabling, the new conditions are seen as enabling.

Williams makes a similar point about Dickens:

> The physical world is never in Dickens unconnected with man. It is of his making, his manufacture, his interpretation. That is why it matters so much what shape he has given it.
>   Dickens' method, in this, relates very precisely to his historical period. It was in just this capacity to remake the world, in the process we summarize as the Industrial Revolution, that men reached this crisis of choice; of the human shape that should underlie the physical creation.[45]

Nowhere is Dickens more positive than in seeing the crowd as more than an amorphous street scene, a crowd of mere passers-by. He overcomes the ambivalence of Baudelaire by at once registering the shock of the crowd and making real the crowd's human shape. Dickens's crowd is not random but in fact manmade, and because it is manmade Dickens can show us its underlying human connections. This is a crowd, then, divested of its mystery; the individual is not a passive recipient of the shock of an alien mass from which he withdraws in horror, or simply a victim of a new circumstance, but actively a participant.[46] Active participation means the immediacy of

45. Williams, *English Novel*, p. 35.
46. The "shock" of the city, although clearly an important fact of life in the Industrial Revolution and after, has nonetheless become a cliché as well as an idea liable to wild exaggeration. The move from country to city meant,

choice, enables choice, and cancels the distance of observation. It is from the vantage point of observation that the crowd shocks. Observation is precisely the distance that the Industrial Revolution bestowed on class. It was the distance of class that required the protective reaction of Bentham's Panopticon.

For Bentham—as for Hazlitt's Mr. Harmer—the method of the Panopticon represented a decisive benevolent intervention. But it is hardly possible to consider this benevolence as a creative response to the shock experience. Dickens's intention—Williams is undoubtedly right about this—was to create a consciousness of relationships and connections so as to cut through the obscuring fog of the streets. To make things clear was also, however, Bentham's aim. The paradox of Dickens is that his method at once reproduces the energy of industrial transformation and the protective retreat of the Panopticon. It is on this basis that I differ from Williams. Dickens's "new kind of novel" was possible, Williams argues, "because he shared with the new urban popular culture certain decisive experiences and responses. That he shared with it, also, certain adjustments and illusions is a significant but minor part of this case."[47] My own reading leads to a different judgment. I

___

as F. S. Schwarzbach says, "profound dislocation," but one is unwilling to assent to his further judgment that "it is . . . by no means inappropriate to compare the experience of entering a life in the early nineteenth century city in England to that of inmates of concentration camps in Germany or communist prisoner-of-war camps in Korea in the early 1950s" (*Dickens and the City*, p. 10). Surely this comparison is extremely inappropriate. In the first place, the Jews and political prisoners herded into the German camps found themselves there after a very different sequence of experiences from those that brought soldiers to the Korean camps. Second, beyond "dislocation," neither of these experiences corresponds to that of entering a nineteenth-century city, especially London. To make one point only: many people found London frightening and even inhuman (and still do); but no groups were brought to London in cattle cars and then threatened with systematic and intentional extermination by means of torture and gas chambers. Schwarzbach's woefully inapt analogies demean and distort both the experience of the camps and the experience of city life.

47. Williams, *English Novel*, p. 28.

believe Dickens responded to the new city in a more thoroughly middle-class way than Williams allows. But, more important, I think the adjustments, illusions, and retreats in Dickens's response are as significant a part of the case as his positive achievement. In the contradictions of his fiction Dickens shows us the contradictions of his society. The structure of feeling he enacts cannot be accurately understood unless we allow that it is precisely the fact of contradiction that defines it.

We can say that the effort to invest the experience of the Industrial Revolution, its experience of transformation, with a kind of aura was—wittingly or not—intended to arrest the creation of a new consciousness. This is the reactionary importance of Macaulay's "Our fields are cultivated . . . ," with its missing agent, and his emphasis on the falsely unitary "man" (see Chapter 2). *Dombey and Son* demystifies Macaulay's euphoric account of "dominion." The activity of "man" is made plainly visible. We know from the novel that Dombey's expropriation of the world for profit, whatever the political economists may say of it, has disastrous human consequences. We know this because Dickens the novelist makes palpable the real connections of life within the pell-mell of the city. Dickens makes available to us this "sensation of the modern age." But the breadth and panorama of his novels do not hide the fact that Dickens is as much an inspector of the crowd as part of it. He picks out individuals from the crowd as Carker picks out Rob in the streets. The whole benevolent intention is qualified at its base by the method of individuation, by the echo in this method of the Panopticon, and by its effect of social control. Dickens demonstrates the contradiction of inspection: his taking off the rooftops enables perception of individuals—real people—in the urban mass, but this perception strips the individual of his or her social identity and of his or her freedom.

We may contrast Dickens with another great urban writer: Hazlitt. In his essay "On Londoners and Country People" Hazlitt notes the distinctive existence of the crowd. He says of the cockney: "There is a glare, a perpetual hubbub, a noise, a crowd about him; he sees and hears a vast number of things, and knows nothing." Hazlitt continues:

It is a strange state of society (such as that in London) where a man does not know his next-door neighbours, and where the feelings (one would think) must recoil upon themselves, and either fester or become obtuse. Mr Wordsworth, in the preface to his poem of the "Excursion," represents men in cities as so many wild beasts or evil spirits, shut up in cells of ignorance, without natural affections, and barricadoed down in sensuality and selfishness. . . . And it would be so, if men were merely cut off from intercourse with their immediate neighbours, and did not meet together generally and more at large. But man in London becomes, as Mr Burke has it, a sort of "public creature." . . . If he witnesses less of the details of private life, he has better opportunities of observing its larger masses and varied movements. He sees the stream of human life pouring along the streets—its comforts and embellishments piled up in the shops—the houses are proof of the industry, the public buildings of the art and magnificence of man. . . . In London there is a *public*, and each man is part of it. We are gregarious, and affect the kind . . . a community of ideas and knowledge (rather than local proximity) is the bond of society and good fellowship. This is the great cause of the tone of political feeling in large and populous cities. . . . We comprehend that vast denomination, the *People*, of which we see a tenth part daily moving before us; and by having our imaginations emancipated from petty interests and personal dependence, we learn to venerate ourselves as men, and to respect the rights of human nature.[48]

There is much here that Dickens makes us experience; we recognize the cells of ignorance, and remember Dickens's confidence that this condition can be overcome. Similarly the vital gregariousness of the Londoner figures centrally in Dickens. But whereas Hazlitt moves from the individual to the mass, and sees this new consciousness of mass as emancipating, as raising a new standard of human nature, on the whole we find

48. *Works*, XII, 76–77; Hazlitt's italics.

the reverse in Dickens. For Hazlitt "in London there is a *public;* and each man is a part of it": the individual identity is strengthened and extended by its place among the crowd of others. But Dickens separates the individual from the mass and shows him or her immersed in petty interests. It is true that he also shows the relationship among the mass of petty interests, but it is in these terms he does so rather than in Hazlitt's. Stephen Blackpool's imagination is not emancipated by his awareness of connections with his fellow workers. It would be easy to conclude, following Hazlitt, that the masses make history, for Hazlitt gives us the awareness to make this idea more than a cliché. But just here Dickens draws back. If he is the great artist of the crowd, he nonetheless does not value it in its own terms as crowd or aggregate or class. When he pays attention to the fact of class, it is to show it up as a kind of tyranny, as in *Hard Times,* or to mock it, as in his satire of Podsnap. Hazlitt, in contrast, affirms the positive new dimensions of mass.

A further paradox of Dickens's individuation is that the energy that enables it is authorial and does not infuse his characters. Williams is persuasive in his demonstration that, for Dickens, the physical world is never unconnected from people but of their making. But if in this way Dickens may be said to show, as it were, the animate history of inanimate objects, the tremendously energetic narrative that creates this significant awareness too often renders the animate inanimate. The consciousness of people creating their social environment is not matched in Dickens by an equally strong consciousness of individuals making their own lives and certainly not by any sense of his fictional characters living out, as characters, a meaningful autonomy. Bounderby, the epitome of the self-made man, is grotesque and hypocritical; and if Walter Gay may be said to make his fortune, how he does so is certainly a mystery to the reader. Instead what we find in Dickens is a whole theater of characters utterly under the author's thumb, their expressions and their phrases fixed; and a handful of

characters struggling, as it were, against a novel's controlling
narrative direction. Perhaps the energy level of Dickens's
novels is so high because he was uniquely aware of the "exces-
sive energies at work in the external world." Perhaps this
concentration of energy in the narrative shield was crucial to
the creation of consciousness that was his purpose, and therefore the price of his achievement was the autonomy of most of
his characters. In any event I think that one explanation for
the notorious difficulty readers have had with definition of
Dickens's method of characterization can be found in this tension between the high level of authorial energy and control
and the contrary reach by his central characters for autonomy.
The method is so abundantly transforming and the display of
connections in the baffling pell-mell of the crowd so illuminating that we may not give due attention to the fact that, at a
certain point, this energy becomes frozen, and characters fail
to gain a fully realized life.

In my view this situation is exacerbated by Dickens's
willingness to employ strictly conventional endings, and to
lend the authority of his narrative energy to a development of
events wholly false in their outcome. Dickens uses the conventions of the novel-as-structure-of-courtship with off-putting
good humor and sentimentality to draw the stories of, say,
Our Mutual Friend and *Dombey and Son* into grotesquely inappropriate finales. These are fairy-tale endings pure and simple. If, as Benjamin says, Baudelaire indicates "the price for
which sensation of the modern world may be had: the disintegration of the aura in the experience of shock," Dickens in
contrast seems very reluctant to acknowledge the necessity to
pay this price. In Dickens we find along with the experience of
shock the need for, or in any event the attempt to retain, the
aura of an anterior experience. There is literal disintegration,
in *Dombey*, in the scenes depicting the construction of the
railway, but then as well the wistful fairy-tale conclusion.
Although such endings do not cancel out the main body of the
novels, neither are they a small matter. I do not think they can

be ignored or explained away. For one thing, they are so well anticipated. These false endings are meticulously plotted. Consequently, if the purpose of Dickens's developed fiction is the creation of consciousness, of recognitions and relationships, as Williams argues, we have to register the fact that his endings and his plots contradict that purpose. They are a kind of deadweight in his fiction, dead places in his creative vision. These dead spots indicate, I believe, a potentially disabling irresolution in Dickens's art as in his society, a dangerous willingness to keep the relics of a disintegrated and anachronistic consciousness actively in place. It was precisely against this tendency, in the society and in the novel, that half a century later D. H. Lawrence wrote in *Lady Chatterley's Lover:*

> It is the way our sympathy flows and recoils that really determines our lives. And here lies the vast importance of the novel, properly handled. It can inform and lead into new places the flow of our sympathetic consciousness, and it can lead our sympathy away in recoil from things gone dead. Therefore, the novel, properly handled, can reveal the most secret places of life: for it's in the *passional* secret places of life, above all, that the tide of sensitive awareness needs to ebb and flow, cleansing and freshening.[49]

In my view the most positive literary responses to the Industrial Revolution occur in *Jane Eyre* and in sections of the later Dickens. Brontë and Dickens create new novels appropriate to a new reality. They demonstrate "the vast importance of the novel" by revealing the "*passional* secret places of life." Dickens is especially creative in his engagement with the crowd. But this creativity harbors a radical doubt of the individual's ability to shape his or her own life. Lawrence, who connects the Industrial Revolution with our own time, raises the standard that allows us at once to appreciate Dickens's achievement and to notice the gaps and the incompleteness in that achievement.

49. D. H. Lawrence, *Lady Chatterley's Lover* (New York: Signet, 1962), p. 94; Lawrence's italics.

I have been writing, in this concluding discussion, of correspondences between the novel and social and ideological history. My emphasis has fallen on structures of feeling that, I hope, illuminate the interrelations between novel and society, or, better, show the novel as a vital practice in the broader response in consciousness to the Industrial Revolution. But it seems appropriate to close, with Lawrence, on a slightly different note. For Lawrence underscores that what matters finally is our awareness of the novel's active role in the active creation of consciousness. The ultimate importance of perceived connections and relationships must lie, as Lawrence says, in their ability to draw us away from things gone dead so that we may most fruitfully participate in the active human creation of human society.

Index

218 INDEX

Macaulay, Thomas Babington,
26–28, 44, 49, 208
Machine breaking. *See* Luddism.
Machinery, 28–29, 32–34, 124, 125,
129–32
in *Shirley*, 134, 141
Mackay, Robert B., 187n
*Making of the English Working Class,
The. See* Thompson, E. P.
Mansfield Park. See Austen, Jane.
Marcus, Steven, 72, 75n
Marriage, 41–44, 159, 166–77
in *Hard Times*, 93–94
in *Jane Eyre*, 82–86, 159
in *Pride and Prejudice*, 159
in *Shirley*, 144–45, 147–55, 158
See also Courtship; Family; Il-
legitimacy.
Martin, Colonel Samuel, 104, 108,
110n
Marx, Karl, 12, 18, 27–28, 44
Mary Barton. See Gaskell, Elizabeth.
Masses, 191–92, 199, 109–10
See also City; Crowd.
Mellor, George, 126
Mob, 128–29, 181
in *Shirley*, 156–57
Moll Flanders (Defoe), 188
Money, 28, 30–31, 35, 59–60, 89,
168
Mudrick, Marvin, 61n, 69n

Namier, Louis, 103–4
Napoleon, 102, 112, 127, 164
Newgate, 179, 183, 183n–84n, 187.
See also Penitentiary.
Nottingham, 124, 127

Offor, Richard, 126n
Our Mutual Friend (Dickens), 176,
211

Panopticon. See Bentham, Jeremy.
Peacock, A. J., 126n
Peel, Frank, 126n, 137–38, 139, 140
Risings of the Luddites, 137–38,
139n

Penitentiary, 182–87
Perceval, Spencer, 102, 127
Persuasion (Austen), 111
Philosophy of Manufactures, The (Ure),
28–29
Political economy, 28–29
Pride and Prejudice. See Austen, Jane.
Proust, Marcel, 200, 202
Punishment, 182–87

Quinlan, Maurice J., 119n

Ragatz, Lowell Joseph, 105–6, 107
*Absentee Ownership in the British
Caribbean*, 105n
*Fall of the Planter Class in the British
Caribbean, The*, 106n, 107n
Rasselas (Johnson), 71
Rawdon, Yorkshire, 124–25, 133n
Reflections on the Revolution in France
(Burke), 119, 120n
Rich, Adrienne, 84n
Richardson, Samuel, 164, 168, 177,
188
Clarissa, 188
Riencourt, Amaury de, 159n
Rigby, Elizabeth, 73, 75
Risings of the Luddites (Peel), 137–38,
139n
Roberson, Reverend Hammond,
141
Robinson, Joan, 30, 34n
Romanticism, 71–72, 75n
Rowbotham, Sheila, 39, 42
Rudé, George, 126n
Rural Rides (Cobbett), 36n, 37
Ruskin, John, 30, 31, 34

Schorer, Mark, 53n
Schwarzbach, F. S., 198n, 207n
Sheridan, Richard B., 103n, 104n,
106n, 108n, 110n, 111
Shirley. See Brontë, Charlotte.
Shorter, Edward, 41n
Simon, Brian, 48
Slavery, 34, 35–36, 106, 110–11

FROM CUSTOM TO CAPITAL

Designed by G. T. Whipple, Jr.
Composed by The Composing Room of Michigan, Inc.
in 11 point VIP Janson, 2 points leaded,
with display lines in Janson.
Printed offset by Thomson/Shore, Inc.
on Warren's Number 66 text, 50 pound basis.
Bound by John H. Dekker & Sons, Inc.
in Holliston book cloth
and stamped in All Purpose foil.